THE MARY FLEXNER LECTURES
OF BRYN MAWR COLLEGE

Notes Toward
a Performative Theory
of Assembly

JUDITH BUTLER

HARVARD UNIVERSITY PRESS

Cambridge, Massachusetts

London, England

2015

Library of Congress Cataloging-in-Publication Data

Butler, Judith, 1956– author.
   Notes toward a performative theory of assembly / Judith Butler.
      pages cm
   Includes bibliographical references and index.
      ISBN 978-0-674-96775-5 (cloth : alk. paper)   1. Assembly, Right
of—Social aspects.   2. Public meetings.   3. Demonstrations.
4. Performative (Philosophy)   I. Title.
   K3256.B88 2015
      323.4'701—dc23   2015014177

THE MARY FLEXNER LECTURESHIP was established at Bryn Mawr College on February 12, 1928, by Bernard Flexner, in honor of his sister, Mary Flexner, a graduate of the College. The income from the endowment is to be used annually or at longer intervals, at the discretion of the Directors of the College, as an honorarium for a distinguished American or foreign scholar in the field of the humanities. The object of the lectureship is to bring to the College scholars of distinction who will be a stimulus to the faculty and students and who will help to maintain the highest ideals and standards of learning.

Contents

Introduction

Since the emergence of mass numbers of people in Tahrir Square in the winter months of 2010, scholars and activists have taken a renewed interest in the form and effect of public assemblies. The issue is at once ancient and timely. Groups suddenly coming together in large numbers can be a source of hope as well as fear, and just as there are always good reasons to fear the dangers of mob action, there are good grounds for discerning political potential in unpredictable assemblies. In a way, democratic theories have always feared "the mob" even as they affirm the importance of expressions of the popular will, even in their unruly form. The literature is vast, and tends to recur to authors as diverse as Edmund Burke and Alexis de Tocqueville, who wondered quite explicitly whether democratic state structures could survive unbridled expressions of popular sovereignty or whether popular rule devolves into the tyranny of the majority. This book will neither review nor adjudicate these important debates in democratic theory, but only suggest that debates about popular demonstrations tend to be governed either by fears of chaos or by radical hope for the future, though sometimes fear and hope get interlocked in complex ways.

I mark these recurrent tensions in democratic theory in order to underscore from the start a certain disjunction between the political form of democracy and the principle of popular sovereignty, since the two are not the same. Indeed, it is important to keep them apart if we are to understand how expressions of the popular will can call into question a particular political form, especially one that calls itself democratic even as its critics question that claim. The principle is simple and well known, but the presumptions at work remain vexing. We could despair of deciding the right form for democracy, and simply concede its polysemy. If democracies are composed of all those political forms that call themselves democratic, or that are regularly called democratic, then we adopt a certain nominalist approach to the matter. But if and when political orders deemed democratic are brought into crisis by an assembled or orchestrated collective that claims to be the popular will, to represent the people along with a prospect of a more real and substantive democracy, then an open battle ensues on the meaning of democracy, one that does not always take the form of a deliberation. Without adjudicating which popular assemblies are "truly" democratic and which are not, we can note from the start that the struggle over "democracy" as a term actively characterizes several political situations. How we name that struggle seems to matter very much, given that sometimes a movement is deemed antidemocratic, even terrorist, and on other occasions or in other contexts, the same movement is understood as a popular effort to realize a more inclusive and substantive democracy. That table can turn quite easily, and when strategic alliances require regarding one group as "terrorist" on one occasion and as "democratic allies" on another, we see that "democracy," considered as an appellation, can be quite easily treated as a strategic discursive term. So, apart from the nominalists who think that democracies are those forms of government called democracies, there are discursive strategists who rely on modes of public discourse, marketing, and propaganda to decide the question of which states and which popular movements will or will not be called democratic.

It is of course tempting to say that a democratic movement is one called by that name, or one that calls itself by that name, but that is to give up on democracy. Although democracy implies the power of self-determination, it hardly follows that any group that determines itself to be representative can rightly claim to be "the people." In January 2015, Pegida (European Patriots Against the Islamicization of the West), an openly anti-immigrant political party in Germany, claimed "we are the people," a self-naming practice that sought precisely to exclude Muslim immigrants from the operative idea of the nation (and it did so by associating itself with a phrase popularized in 1989, casting now a darker meaning on the "unification" of Germany). Angela Merkel responded, "Islam is part of Germany," at about the same time that Pegida's leader, exposed as having dressed up like Hitler for a photo shoot, was compelled to resign. A row like this graphically raises the question, who really are "the people"? And what operation of discursive power circumscribes "the people" at any given moment, and for what purpose?

"The people" are not a given population, but are rather constituted by the lines of demarcation that we implicitly or explicitly establish. As result, as much as we need to test whether any given way of positing "the people" is inclusive, we can only indicate excluded populations through a further demarcation. Self-constitution becomes especially problematic to consider under these conditions. Not every discursive effort to establish who "the people" are works. The assertion is often a wager, a bid for hegemony. So when a group or assembly or orchestrated collectivity calls itself "the people," they wield discourse in a certain way, making presumptions about who is included and who is not, and so unwittingly refer to a population who is not "the people." Indeed, when the struggle over deciding who belongs to "the people" gets intense, one group opposes its own version of "the people" to those who are outside, those considered to threaten "the people," or to oppose the proposed version of "the people." As a result, we have (a) those who seek to define the people (a group much smaller than the people they seek to define), (b) the people defined (and demarcated) in the course of that discursive wager, (c) the people who are not "the people," and (d) those who are trying to establish that last group as part of the people. Even when we say "everyone" in an effort to posit an all-inclusive group, we are still making implicit assumptions about who is included, and so we hardly overcome what Chantal Mouffe and Ernesto Laclau so aptly describe as "the constitutive exclusion" by which any particular notion of inclusion is established.[1]

The body politic is posited as a unity it can never be. Yet, that does not have to be a cynical conclusion. Those who in a spirit of realpolitik reckon that since every formation of "the people" is partial, we should simply accept that partiality as a fact of politics, are clearly opposed by those who seek to expose and oppose those forms of exclusion, often knowing quite well that full inclusiveness is not possible, but for whom the struggle is ongoing. The reasons for this are at least twofold: on the one hand, many exclusions are made without knowledge that they are being made, since exclusion is often naturalized, taken to be "the state of things" and not an explicit problem; secondly, inclusiveness is not the only aim of democratic politics, especially radical democratic politics. Of course, it is true that any version of "the people" that excludes some of the people is not inclusive and, therefore, not representative. But it is also true that every determination of "the people" involves an act of demarcation that draws a line, usually on the basis of nationality or against the background of the nation-state, and that line immediately becomes a contentious border. In other words, there is no possibility of "the people" without a discursive border drawn somewhere, either traced along the lines of existing nation-states, racial or linguistic communities, or political affiliation. The discursive move to establish "the people" in one way or another is a bid to have a certain border recognized, whether we understand that as a border of a nation or as the frontier of that class of people to be considered "recognizable" as a people.

So one reason inclusiveness is not the only aim of democracy, especially radical democracy, is that democratic politics has to be concerned with who counts as "the people," how the demarcation is enacted that brings to the fore who "the people" are and that consigns to the background, to the margin, or to oblivion those people who do not count as "the people." The point of a democratic politics is not simply to extend recognition equally to all of the people, but, rather, to grasp that only by changing the relation between the recognizable and unrecognizable can (a) equality be understood and pursued and (b) "the people" become open to a further elaboration. Even when a form of recognition is extended to all the people, there remains an active premise that there is a vast region of those who remain unrecognizable, and that very power differential is reproduced every time that form of recognition is extended. Paradoxically, as certain forms of recognition are extended, the region of the unrecognizable is preserved and expanded accordingly. The conclusion is that these explicit and implicit forms of inequality that are sometimes reproduced by fundamental categories such as inclusion and recognition have to be addressed as part of a temporally open democratic struggle. The same can be said about those implicit and explicit forms of contentious border politics that are raised by some of the most elementary and taken-for-granted forms of referring to the people, the populace, and the popular will. In effect, the insight into persistent exclusion forces us back into the process of naming and renaming, of renewing what we mean by "the people" and what various people mean when they invoke that term.

The problem of demarcation introduces another dimension to the problem, since not all of the related discursive actions that go into recognizing and misrecognizing the people are explicit. The operation of their power is to some extent performative. That is, they enact certain political distinctions, including inequality and exclusion, without always naming them. When we say that inequality is "effectively" reproduced when "the people" are only partially recognizable, or even "fully" recognizable within restrictively national terms, then we are claiming that the positing of "the people" does more than simply name who the people are. The act of delimitation operates according to a *performative* form of power that establishes a fundamental problem of democracy even as—or precisely when—it furnishes its key term, "the people."

We could linger longer with this discursive problem, since there is an always-open question of whether "the people" are the same as those who express "the popular will" and whether those acts of self-naming qualify as self-determination or even valid expressions of the popular will. The concept of self-determination is also here at play, and so implicitly the very idea of popular sovereignty. As important as it is to clarify this lexicon of democratic theory—especially in light of recent debates about whether any of the public assemblies and demonstrations we have seen in the Arab Spring, the Occupy Movement, or the antiprecarity demonstrations—and to ask whether such movements can be interpreted as true or promising examples of the popular will, the will of the people, the suggestion of this text is that we have to read such scenes not only in terms of the version of the people they explicitly set forth, but the relations of power by which they are enacted.[2] Such enactments are invariably transitory when they remain extraparliamentary. And when they realize new parliamentary forms, they risk losing their character as the popular will. Popular assemblies form unexpectedly and dissolve under voluntary or involuntary conditions, and this transience is, I would suggest, bound up with their "critical" function. As much as collective expressions of the popular will can call into question the legitimacy of a government that claims to represent the people, they can also lose themselves in the forms of government that they support and institute. At the same time, governments come into being and pass away sometimes by virtue of actions on the part of the people, so those concerted actions are similarly transient, consisting of the withdrawal of support, deconstituting the government's claim on legitimacy, but also constituting new forms. As the popular will persists in the forms it institutes, it must also fail to lose itself in those forms if it is to retain the right to withdraw its support from any political form that fails to maintain legitimacy.

How, then, do we think about these transient and critical gatherings? One important argument that follows is that it matters that bodies assemble, and that the political meanings enacted by demonstrations are not only those that are enacted by discourse, whether written or vocalized. Embodied actions of various kinds signify in ways that are, strictly speaking, neither discursive nor prediscursive. In other words, forms of assembly already signify prior to, and apart from, any particular demands they make. Silent gatherings, including vigils or funerals, often signify in excess of any particular written or vocalized account of what they are about. These forms of embodied and plural performativity are important components of any understanding of "the people" even as they are necessarily partial. Not everyone can appear in a bodily form, and many of those who cannot appear, who are constrained from appearing or who operate through virtual or digital networks, are also part of "the people," defined precisely by being constrained from making a specific bodily appearance in public space, which compels us to reconsider the restrictive ways "the public sphere" has been uncritically posited by those who assume full access and rights of appearance on a designated platform. A second sense of enactment, then, emerges here in light of embodied forms of action and mobility that signify in excess of whatever is said. If we consider why freedom of assembly is separate from freedom of expression, it is precisely because the power that people have to gather together is itself an important political prerogative, quite distinct from the right to say whatever they have to say once people have gathered. The gathering signifies in excess of what is said, and that mode of signification is a concerted bodily enactment, a plural form of performativity.

We might be tempted on the basis of older habits to say, "but if it signifies, it is surely discursive," and maybe that is true. But that rejoinder, even if it holds, does not let us examine that important chiasmic relation between forms of linguistic performativity and forms of bodily performativity. They overlap; they are not altogether distinct; they are not, however, identical with one another. As Shoshana Felman has shown, even the speech act is implicated in the embodied conditions of life.[3] Vocalization requires a larynx or a technological prosthetic. And sometimes what one signifies by the means of expression is quite different from what is explicitly owned as the aim of the speech act itself. If performativity has often been associated with individual performance, it may prove important to reconsider those forms of performativity that only operate through forms of coordinated action, whose condition and aim is the reconstitution of plural forms of agency and social practices of resistances. So this movement or stillness, this parking of my body in the middle of another's action, is neither my act nor yours, but something that happens by virtue of the relation between us, arising from that relation, equivocating between the I and the we, seeking at once to preserve and disseminate the generative value of that equivocation, an active and deliberately sustained relation, a collaboration distinct from hallucinatory merging or confusion.

THE SPECIFIC THESIS OF THIS BOOK is that acting in concert can be an embodied form of calling into question the inchoate and powerful dimensions of reigning notions of the political. The embodied character of this questioning works in at least two ways: on the one hand, contestations are enacted by assemblies, strikes, vigils, and the occupation of public spaces; on the other hand, those bodies are the object of many of the demonstrations that take precarity as their galvanizing condition. After all, there is an indexical force of the body that arrives with other bodies in a zone visible to media coverage: it is *this* body, and *these* bodies, that require employment, shelter, health care, and food, as well as a sense of a future that is not the future of unpayable debt; it is *this* body, or *these* bodies, or bodies *like* this body or these bodies, that live the condition of an imperiled livelihood, decimated infrastructure, accelerating precarity.

In some ways my aim is to stress the obvious under conditions in which the obvious is vanishing: there are ways of expressing and demonstrating precarity that importantly engage embodied action and forms of expressive freedom that belong more properly to public assembly. Some critics have argued that the Occupy movements succeeded only in bringing people out onto the streets, and facilitated the occupation of spaces whose public status is contested by expanding privatization. Sometimes those spaces are contested because they are, quite literally, being sold off as property to private investors (Gezi Park in Istanbul). But other times those spaces are closed to public assemblies in the name of "security" or even "public health." The explicit aims of those assemblies vary: opposition to despotic rule, securitarian regimes, nationalism, militarism, economic injustice, unequal rights of citizenship, statelessness, ecological damage, the intensification of economic inequality and the acceleration of precarity. Sometimes an assembly seeks explicitly to challenge capitalism itself or neoliberalism, considered as a new development or variant, or, in Europe, austerity measures, or, in Chile as elsewhere, the potential destruction of public higher education.[4]

Of course, these are different assemblies, and different alliances, and I do not believe that one can come up with a single account of these most recent forms of public demonstrations and occupations that link them more broadly to the history and principle of public assembly. They are not all permutations of the multitude, but neither are they so disconnected that we can draw no ties among them. A social and legal historian would have to do some of that comparative work—and I hope they continue to do so in light of recent forms of assembly. From my more limited vantage point, I want to suggest only that when bodies assemble on the street, in the square, or in other forms of public space (including virtual ones) they are exercising a plural and performative right to appear, one that asserts and instates the body in the midst of the political field, and which, in its expressive and signifying function, delivers a bodily demand for a more livable set of economic, social, and political conditions no longer afflicted by induced forms of precarity.

In this time in which neoliberal economics increasingly structures public services and institutions, including schools and universities, in a time in which people are losing their homes, their pensions, and their prospects for work in increasing numbers, we are faced in a new way with the idea that some populations are considered disposable.[5] There is short-term work or no work at all, or post-Fordist forms of flexible labor that rely on the substitutability and dispensability of working peoples. These developments, bolstered by prevailing attitudes toward health insurance and social security, suggest that market rationality is deciding whose health and life should be protected and whose health and life should not. Of course, there are differences between policies that explicitly seek the deaths of certain populations and policies that produce conditions of systematic negligence that effectively let people die. Foucault helped us to articulate this distinction when he spoke about the very specific strategies of biopower, the management of life and death in ways that no longer require a sovereign who explicitly decides and enforces the question of who will live and who will die.[6] And Achille Mbembe has elaborated upon this distinction with his conception of "necropolitics."

And this was, for some of us, keenly exemplified at that meeting of the Tea Party in the United States in which Congressman Ron Paul suggested that those who have serious illness and cannot pay for health insurance, or "choose" not to pay, as he would put it, would simply have to die. A shout of joy rippled through the crowd, according to published reports. It was, I conjecture, the kind of joyous shout that usually accompanies going to war or forms of nationalist fervor. But if this was for some a joyous occasion, it must have been fueled by a belief that those who do not make sufficient wages or who are not in secure enough employment do not deserve to be covered by health care, and a belief that none of the rest of us are responsible for those people. The implication was clearly that those who are not able to achieve jobs with health care belong to a population that deserves to die and that is finally responsible for their own death.

Shocking for many people who still live under the nominal framework of social democracy is the underlying presumption that individuals ought to care only for themselves, and not for others, and that health care is not a public good, but a commodity. In this same speech, Paul praises the traditional function of the church and charity for taking care of the needy. Although some Christian-left alternatives to this situation have emerged in Europe and elsewhere to make sure that those abandoned by forms of social welfare are taken care of by philanthropic or communitarian practices of "care," those alternatives often supplement and support the decimation of public services such as health care. In other words, they accept the new role for Christian ethics and practices (and Christian hegemony) that the decimation of basic social services provides. Something similar happens in Palestine when the infrastructural conditions of life are constantly being destroyed by bombing, water rationing, the uprooting of olive groves, and the dismantling of established irrigation systems. This destruction is ameliorated by nongovernmental organizations that reestablish roads and shelters, but the destruction does not change; the NGO interventions presume that the destruction will continue, and understand their task as repairing and ameliorating those conditions between bouts of destruction. A macabre rhythm develops between the tasks of destruction and the tasks of renewal or reconstruction (often opening up temporary market potential as well), all of which supports the normalization of the occupation. Of course, this does not mean that there should be no effort to repair homes and streets, to provide better irrigation and more water, and to replant destroyed olive groves, or that NGOs have no role. Their role is crucial. And yet, if those tasks take the place of a more thoroughgoing opposition to occupation that brings about its end, they risk becoming practices that make occupation functional.

What about that sadistic shout of joy emerging from that Tea Party meeting, translating into the idea that those who cannot find their way to gain access to health care will rightly contract diseases, or suffer accidents, and will rightly die as a consequence? Under what economic and political conditions do such joyous forms of cruelty emerge and make their sentiments known? Do we want to call this a death wish? I start with the presupposition that something has gone very wrong, or has been wrong for a long time, when the idea of the death of an impoverished or uninsured person elicits shouts of joy from a proponent of Tea Party republicanism, a nationalist variant of economic libertarianism that has fully eclipsed any sense of a common social responsibility with a colder and more calculating metric aided and abetted, it seems, by a rather joyous relation to cruelty.

Although "responsibility" is a word that is often found circulating among those who defend neoliberalism and renewed versions of political and economic individualism, I will be seeking to reverse and renew its meaning in the context of thinking about collective forms of assembly. It is not easy to defend a notion of ethics, including key notions such as freedom and responsibility, in the face of their discursive appropriation. For if, according to those who value the decimation of social services, we are each responsible only for ourselves, and certainly not for others, and if responsibility is first and foremost a responsibility to become economically self-sufficient under conditions that undermine all prospects of self-sufficiency, then we are confronted by a contradiction that can easily drive one mad: we are morally pushed to become precisely the kind of subjects who are structurally foreclosed from realizing that norm. Neoliberal rationality demands self-sufficiency as a moral ideal at the same time that neoliberal forms of power work to destroy that very possibility at an economic level, establishing every member of the population as potentially or actually precarious, even using the ever-present threat of precarity to justify its heightened regulation of public space and its deregulation of market expansion. The minute one proves oneself to be incapable of conforming to the norm of self-sufficiency (for instance when one cannot pay health care or take advantage of privatized care), one becomes potentially dispensable. And then, this dispensable creature is addressed by a political morality that demands individualistic responsibility or that operates on a model of the privatization of "care."

Indeed, we are in the midst of a biopolitical situation in which diverse populations are increasingly subject to what is called "precaritization."[7] Usually induced and reproduced by governmental and economic institutions, this process acclimatizes populations over time to insecurity and hopelessness; it is structured into the institutions of temporary labor and decimated social services and the general attrition of the active remnants of social democracy in favor of entrepreneurial modalities supported by fierce ideologies of individual responsibility and the obligation to maximize one's own market value as the ultimate aim in life.[8] In my view, this important process of precaritization has to be supplemented by an understanding of precarity as effecting a change in psychic reality, as Lauren Berlant has suggested in her theory of affect;[9] it implies a heightened sense of expendability or disposability that is differentially distributed throughout society. The more one complies with the demand of "responsibility" to become self-reliant, the more socially isolated one becomes and the more precarious one feels; and the more supporting social structures fall away for "economic" reasons, the more isolated one feels in one's sense of heightened anxiety and "moral failure." It involves an escalation of anxiety about one's future and those who may be dependent on one; it imposes a frame of individual responsibility on the person suffering that anxiety; and it redefines responsibility as the demand to become an entrepreneur of oneself under conditions that make that dubious vocation impossible.

So one question that emerges for us here is the following: What function does public assembly serve in the context of this form of "responsibilization," and what opposing form of ethics does it embody and express? Over and against an increasingly individualized sense of anxiety and failure, public assembly embodies the insight that this is a social condition both shared and unjust, and that assembly enacts a provisional and plural form of coexistence that constitutes a distinct ethical and social alternative to "responsibilization." As I hope to suggest, these forms of assembly can be understood as nascent and provisional versions of popular sovereignty. They can also be regarded as indispensable reminders of how legitimation functions in democratic theory and practice. This assertion of plural existence is not in any way a triumph over all forms of precarity, though it articulates, through its enactments, an opposition to induced precarity and its accelerations.

The fantasy of the individual capable of undertaking entrepreneurial self-making under conditions of accelerating precarity, if not destitution, makes the uncanny assumption that people can, and must, act in autonomous ways under conditions where life has become unlivable. The thesis of this book is that none of us acts without the conditions to act, even though sometimes we must act to install and preserve those very conditions. The paradox is obvious, and yet what we can see when the precarious assemble is a form of action that demands the conditions for acting and living. What conditions such actions? And how is plural and embodied action to be reconceived within such an historical situation?

Before we turn to these central questions, let us first consider how this contradictory imperative operates in yet other domains. If we consider the rationale for militarization that is based on the claim that "the people" who belong to the nation must be defended, we find that only some of the people are defensible, and that an operative distinction is at work between the defensible and the indefensible, differentiating the people from the population. Precarity shows itself in the midst of this imperative to "defend the people." The military defense requires and institutes precarity not only among those it targets, but also among those it recruits. At least those conscripted into the U.S. Army are promised skills, training, and work, but they are often sent into zones of conflict where there is no clear mandate and where their bodies can be maimed, their psychic lives traumatized, and their lives destroyed. On the one hand, they are considered "indispensable" to the defense of the nation. On the other hand, they are designated as a dispensable population. Even though their deaths are sometimes glorified, they are still dispensable: people to be sacrificed in the name of the people.[10] An operative contradiction is clearly at work: the body that seeks to defend the country is often physically and psychically eviscerated in the course of doing its job. In this way, in the name of defending people, the nation kicks some of its people to the curb. The body instrumentalized for the purposes of "defense" is nevertheless disposable in the course of providing that "defense." Left defenseless in the course of defending the nation, such a body is both indispensable and dispensable. The imperative to provide "the defense of the people" thus requires the dispensability and defenselessness of those tasked with defense.

Of course we are right to distinguish among kinds of protest, differentiating antimilitarization movements from precarity movements, Black Lives Matter from demands for public education. At the same time, precarity seems to run through a variety of such movements, whether it is the precarity of those killed in war, those who lack basic infrastructure, those who are exposed to disproportionate violence on the street, or those who seek to gain an education at the cost of unpayable debt. Sometimes a gathering takes place in the name of the living body, one entitled to life and persistence, even flourishing. At the same time, no matter what the protest is about, it is also, implicitly, a demand to be able to gather, to assemble, and to do so freely without fear of police violence or political censorship. So though the body in its struggle with precarity and persistence is at the heart of so many demonstrations, it is also the body that is on the line, exhibiting its value and its freedom in the demonstration itself, enacting, by the embodied form of the gathering, a claim to the political.

ASSERTING THAT A GROUP OF PEOPLE is still existing, taking up space and obdurately living, is already an expressive action, a politically significant event, and that can happen wordlessly in the course of an unpredictable and transitory gathering. Another "effective" result of such plural enactments is that they make manifest the understanding that a situation is shared, contesting the individualizing morality that makes a moral norm of economic self-sufficiency precisely under conditions when self-sufficiency is becoming increasingly unrealizable. Showing up, standing, breathing, moving, standing still, speech, and silence are all aspects of a sudden assembly, an unforeseen form of political performativity that puts livable life at the forefront of politics. And this seems to be happening before any group lays out its demands or begins to explain itself in proper political speech. Taking place outside of parliamentary modes of written and spoken contributions, the provisional assembly still makes a call for justice. But to understand this "call," we have to ask whether it is right that verbalization remains the norm for thinking about expressive political action. Indeed, we have to rethink the speech act in order to understand what is made and what is done by certain kinds of bodily enactments: the bodies assembled "say" we are not disposable, even if they stand silently. This expressive possibility is part of plural and embodied performativity that we have to understand as marked by dependency and resistance. Assembled creatures such as these depend upon a set of living and institutional processes, infrastructural conditions, to persist and to assert together a right to the conditions of its persistence. That right is part of a broader call to justice, one that may well be articulated by a silent and collective stand. However important words are for such a stand, they do not exhaust the political importance of plural and embodied action.

As much as an assembly can signify a form of popular will, even lay claim to "the" popular will, signifying the indispensable condition of state legitimacy, assemblies are orchestrated by states for the very purpose of flashing before the media the popular support they ostensibly enjoy. In other words, the signifying effect of the assembly, its legitimation effect, can function precisely through orchestrated enactments and orchestrated media coverage, reducing and framing the circulation of the "popular" as a strategy of the state's self-legitimation. Since there is no popular will that exercises its legitimating effect being demarcated or produced within a frame, the struggle over legitimation invariably takes place in the play between public enactments and media images, where state-controlled spectacles do battle with cell phone and social networks to cover an event and its significance. The filming of police actions has become a key way to expose the state-sponsored coercion under which freedom of assembly currently operates. One can easily arrive at a cynical conclusion: it is all a play of images. But perhaps a much more important insight is at stake here, namely, that "the people" are not just produced by their vocalized claims, but also by the conditions of possibility of their appearance, and so within the visual field, and by their actions, and so as part of embodied performance. Those conditions of appearance include infrastructural conditions of staging as well as technological means of capturing and conveying a gathering, a coming together, in the visual and acoustic fields. The sound of what they speak, or the graphic sign of what is spoken, is as important to the activity of self-constitution in the public sphere (and the constitution of the public sphere as a condition of appearance) as any other means. If the people are constituted through a complex interplay of performance, image, acoustics, and all the various technologies engaged in those productions, then "media" is not just reporting who the people claim to be, but media has entered into the very definition of the people. It does not simply assist that definition, or make it possible; it is the stuff of self-constitution, the site of the hegemonic struggle over who "we" are. Of course, we have to study those occasions in which the official frame is dismantled by rival images, or where a single set of images sets off an implacable division in society, or where the numbers of people gathering in resistance overwhelm the frame by which their size is supposed to be cut, or their claim is transformed into uncivil noise. Such gatherings are not the same as democracy itself. We cannot point to one provisional and transient gathering and say, "that is democracy in action," and mean that everything we expect of democracy is emblematized or enacted at such a moment. Gatherings are necessarily transient, and that transience is linked to their critical function. One could say, "but oh, they do not last," and sink into a sense of futility; but that sense of loss is countered by the anticipation of what may be coming: "they could happen at any time!" Gatherings such as these serve as one of democracy's incipient or "fugitive" moments.[11] The demonstrations against precarity may well prove to be a case in point.

As I began to clarify in *Frames of War,* precarity is not simply an existential truth—each of us could find ourselves subject to deprivation, injury, illness, debilitation, or death by virtue of events or processes outside of our control.[12] We are all unknowing and exposed to what may happen, and our not knowing is a sign that we do not, cannot, control all the conditions that constitute our lives. However invariable such a general truth may be, it is lived differentially, since exposure to injury at work, or faltering social services, clearly affects workers and the unemployed much more than others.

On the one hand, everyone is dependent on social relations and enduring infrastructure in order to maintain a livable life, so there is no getting rid of that dependency. On the other hand, that dependency, though not the same as a condition of subjugation, can easily become one. The dependency of human creatures on sustaining and supporting infrastructural life shows that the organization of infrastructure is intimately tied with an enduring sense of individual life: how life is endured, and with what degree of suffering, livability, or hope.

In other words, no one person suffers a lack of shelter without there being a social failure to organize shelter in such a way that it is accessible to each and every person. And no one person suffers unemployment without there being a system or a political economy that fails to safeguard against that possibility. This means that in some of our most vulnerable experiences of social and economic deprivation, what is revealed is not only our precariousness as individual persons—though that may well be revealed—but also the failures and inequalities of socioeconomic and political institutions. In our individual vulnerability to a precarity that is socially induced, each "I" potentially sees how its unique sense of anxiety and failure has been implicated all along in a broader social world. This initiates the possibility of taking apart that individualizing and maddening form of responsibility in favor of an ethos of solidarity that would affirm mutual dependency, dependency on workable infrastructures and social networks, and open the way to a form of improvisation in the course of devising collective and institutional ways of addressing induced precarity.

The chapters of this book seek first to understand the expressive or signifying function of improvisational forms of public assembly, but also to interrogate what counts as "public" and who "the people" may be. By "expressive" I do not mean to imply that some already established sense of the people is expressed through forms of public gathering, but only that just as free speech is considered an "expressive freedom," so, too, is freedom of assembly: some matter of political significance is being enacted and conveyed. This inquiry is situated within a historical time in which the question emerges: How is precarity enacted and opposed in sudden assemblies? To the extent that forms of interdependency are foregrounded in such assemblies, they provide a chance to reflect upon the embodied character of social action and expression, what we might understand as embodied and plural performativity. An ethical conception of human relationality traverses a political analysis throughout these pages and becomes most salient in the discussion of Hannah Arendt on cohabitation and the Levinasian proposition that an ethical demand is in some sense prior to the formation of the choosing subject, and so precedes conventionally liberal notions of contract.

The first chapters focus on forms of assembly that presume modes of belonging and site-specific occasions for political demonstrations, whereas the last chapters ask about forms of ethical obligation that hold among those who do not share a geographical or linguistic sense of belonging. Finally, in taking up Adorno's formulation that it is not possible to live a good life in a bad life, I suggest that the "life" one has to lead is always a social life, implicating us in a larger social, economic, and infrastructural world that exceeds our perspective and the situated, first-person modality of ethical questioning. For this reason, I argue that ethical questions are invariably implicated in social and economic ones, although they are not extinguished by those concerns. Indeed, the very conception of human action as pervasively conditioned implies that when we ask the basic ethical and political question, how ought I to act, we implicitly reference the conditions of the world that make that act possible or, as is increasingly the case under conditions of precarity, that undermine the conditions of acting. What does it mean to act together when the conditions for acting together are devastated or falling away? Such an impasse can become the paradoxical condition of a form of social solidarity both mournful and joyful, a gathering enacted by bodies under duress or in the name of duress, where the gathering itself signifies persistence and resistance.

Chapter 1

Gender Politics and the Right to Appear

Originally, I had given the "title" *Bodies in Alliance* for the original set of lectures at Bryn Mawr College in 2011 that provided the rudiments for this text. It was a timely title, it turns out, although the moment that I came up with it was one in which I could not have known how the title's meaning would play out in time, assume another shape and force. So there we were, gathered in that academic setting as people were gathering across the United States and several other nations to contest various issues, including despotic rule and economic injustice, sometimes challenging capitalism itself, or some of its contemporary forms. And other times, and possibly at the same time, amassing in public together in order to be seen and heard as a plural political presence and force.

We might see these mass demonstrations as a collective rejection of socially and economically induced precarity. More than that, however, what we are seeing when bodies assemble on the street, in the square, or in other public venues is the exercise—one might call it performative—of the right to appear, a bodily demand for a more livable set of lives.

However problematically the notion of "responsibility" has been reappropriated for neoliberal purposes, the concept remains a crucial feature of the critique of accelerating inequality. In the neoliberal morality, each of us is only responsible for ourselves, and not for others, and that responsibility is first and foremost a responsibility to become economically self-sufficient under conditions when self-sufficiency is structurally undermined. Those who cannot afford to pay for health care constitute but one version of a population deemed disposable. And all those who see the increasing gap between rich and poor, who understand themselves to have lost several forms of security and promise, they also understand themselves as abandoned by a government and a political economy that clearly augments wealth for the very few at the expense of the general population. So when people amass on the street, one implication seems clear: they are still here and still there; they persist; they assemble, and so manifest the understanding that their situation is shared, or the beginning of such an understanding. And even when they are not speaking or do not present a set of negotiable demands, the call for justice is being enacted: the bodies assembled "say" "we are not disposable," whether or not they are using words at the moment; what they say, as it were, is "we are still here, persisting, demanding greater justice, a release from precarity, a possibility of a livable life."

To demand justice is, of course, a strong thing to do—it also immediately involves every activist in a philosophical problem: What is justice, and what are the means through which the demand for justice can be made, understood, taken up? The reason it is sometimes said that there are "no demands" when bodies assemble in this way and for this purpose is that the list of demands would not exhaust the meaning of justice that is being demanded. In other words, we can all imagine just solutions to health care, public education, housing, and the distribution and availability of food—that is, we could itemize the injustices in the plural, and present them as a set of specific demands. But perhaps the demand for justice is present in each of those demands, but also necessarily exceeds them. This is clearly a Platonic point, but we do not have to subscribe to a theory of Forms to see other ways in which it operates. For when bodies gather as they do to express their indignation and to enact their plural existence in public space, they are also making broader demands: they are demanding to be recognized, to be valued, they are exercising a right to appear, to exercise freedom, and they are demanding a livable life. Of course, there have to be conditions under which such a claim is registered as a claim. And with the public demonstrations in Ferguson, Missouri, in the summer of 2014, it is easy to see how quickly forms of public political opposition—in this case opposition to the police killing of an unarmed black man, Michael Brown—are quickly renamed as "unrest" or "riots."[1] The concerted actions of groups for the purpose of opposing state violence are understood in these instances as violent action, even when they do not engage in violent acts. How do we understand the form of signification that such protests seek to convey in relation to how they are named by those they oppose? Is this a political form of enacted and plural performativity, the workings of which requires its own consideration?

A QUESTION OFTEN POSED TO ME is the following: How does one move from a theory of gender performativity to a consideration of precarious lives? Although sometimes the question is looking for a biographical answer, it is still a theoretical concern—what is the connection between these two concepts, if there is one? It seems that I was concerned with queer theory and the rights of sexual and gender minorities, and now I am writing more generally about the ways in which war or other social conditions designate certain populations as ungrievable. In *Gender Trouble* (1989) it sometimes seemed that certain acts that individuals could perform would or could have a subversive effect on gender norms. Now I am working the question of alliances among various minorities or populations deemed disposable; more specifically, I am concerned with how precarity—that middle term and, in some ways, that mediating term—might operate, or is operating, as a site of alliance among groups of people who do not otherwise find much in common and between whom there is sometimes even suspicion and antagonism. One political point probably has remained pretty much the same even as my own focus has shifted, and that is that identity politics fails to furnish a broader conception of what it means, politically, to live together, across differences, sometimes in modes of unchosen proximity, especially when living together, however difficult it may be, remains an ethical and political imperative. Moreover, freedom is more often than not exercised with others, not necessarily in a unified or conformist way. It does not exactly presume or produce a collective identity, but a set of enabling and dynamic relations that include support, dispute, breakage, joy, and solidarity.

To understand this dynamic, I propose to investigate two realms of theory abbreviated by the terms "performativity" and "precarity" in order then to suggest how we might consider the right to appear as a coalitional framework, one that links gender and sexual minorities with precarious populations more generally. Performativity characterizes first and foremost that characteristic of linguistic utterances that in the moment of making the utterance makes something happen or brings some phenomenon into being. J. L. Austin is responsible for the term, but it has gone through many revisions and alterations, especially in the work of Jacques Derrida, Pierre Bourdieu, and Eve Kosofsky Sedgwick, to name but a few.[2] An utterance brings what it states into being (illocutionary) or makes a set of events happen as a consequence of the utterance being made (perlocutionary). Why would people be interested in this relatively obscure theory of speech acts? In the first instance, it seems, performativity is a way of naming a power language has to bring about a new situation or to set into motion a set of effects. It is no accident that God is generally credited with the first performative: "Let there be light," and then suddenly light there is. Or presidents who declare war usually do see wars materialize as a result of their declaration, just as judges who pronounce two people married usually also, under the right legal conditions, produce married couples as a result of their utterances. The point is not only that language acts, but that it acts powerfully. So how, then, does a performative theory of speech acts become a performative theory of gender? In the first place, there are usually medical professionals who declare a wailing infant to be a boy or a girl, and even if their utterance is not audible above the din, the box they check is surely legible on the legal documents that get registered with the state. My wager is that most of us have had our genders established by virtue of someone checking a box and sending it in, although in some cases, especially for those with intersexed conditions, it might have taken a while to check the box, or the check may have been erased a few times, or the letter may have been delayed before it was sent. In any case, there was doubtless a graphic event that inaugurated gender for the vast majority of us, or perhaps someone simply exclaimed into the air, "it's a boy" or "it's a girl" (although sometimes that first exclamation is surely a question: someone, dreaming only of having a boy, can only ask one question, "is it a boy?"). Or if we are adopted, someone who decides to consider adopting us has to check off the gender preference, or has to agree to the gender that we are before they can proceed. In some ways, these all remain discursive moments at the inception of our gendered lives. And rarely was there really one person who decided our fate—the idea of a sovereign power with extraordinary linguistic powers has been for the most part replaced by a more diffuse and complicated set of discursive and institutional powers.

So, then, if performativity was considered linguistic, how do *bodily acts* become performative? This is a question we have to ask to understand the formation of gender, but also the performativity of mass demonstrations. In the case of gender, those primary inscriptions and interpellations come with the expectations and fantasies of others that affect us in ways that are at first uncontrollable: this is the psychosocial imposition and slow inculcation of norms. They arrive when we can scarcely expect them, and they make their way with us, animating and structuring our own forms of responsiveness. Such norms are not simply imprinted on us, marking and branding us like so many passive recipients of a culture machine. They also "produce" us, but not in the sense of bringing us into being, nor in the sense of strictly determining who we are. Rather, they inform the lived modes of embodiment we acquire over time, and those very modes of embodiment can prove to be ways of contesting those norms, even breaking with them.

One example of how that happens most clearly is when we reject the terms of gender assignment; indeed, we may well embody or enact that rejection prior to putting our views into words. Indeed, we may know that rejection first as a visceral refusal to conform to the norms relayed by gender assignment. Although we are in some ways obligated to reproduce the norms of gender, the police who oversee our compliance with that obligation are sometimes falling asleep on the job. And we find ourselves veering from the designated path, doing that partially in the dark, wondering whether we did on some occasion act like a girl, or act like enough of a girl, or act enough like a boy, or whether boyness is well exemplified by the boy we are supposed to be, or whether we have somehow missed the mark, and find ourselves dwelling either happily or not so happily between the established categories of gender. The possibility of missing the mark is always there in the enactment of gender; in fact, gender may be that enactment in which missing the mark is a defining feature. There is an ideality, if not a phantasmic dimension to cultural norms of gender, and even as emerging humans seek to reiterate and accommodate those norms, they surely also become aware of a persistent gap between those ideals—many of which conflict with one another—and our various lived efforts at embodiment, where our own understanding and the understanding of others are at cross purposes. If gender first comes to us as someone else's norm, it resides within us as a fantasy that is at once formed by others and also part of my formation.

But my point here, at least, is somewhat simple: gender is received, but surely not simply inscribed on our bodies as if we were merely a passive slate obligated to bear a mark. But what we are at first obligated to do is enact the gender that we are assigned, and that involves, at an unknowing level, being formed by a set of foreign fantasies that are relayed through interpellations of various kinds. And though gender is enacted, time and again, the enactment is not always in compliance with certain kinds of norms, surely not always in precise conformity with the norm. There may be a problem deciphering the norm (there may be several conflicting demands relaying which version of gender is to be achieved, and through what means), but there may be something about enacting a norm that holds within it the possibility of noncompliance. Although gender norms precede us and act upon us (that is one sense of their enactment), we are obligated to reproduce them, and when we do begin, always unwittingly, to reproduce them, something may always go awry (and that is a second sense of their enactment). And yet, in the course of this reproduction, some weakness of the norm is revealed, or another set of cultural conventions intervenes to produce confusion or conflict within a field of norms, or, in the midst of our enactment, another desire starts to govern, and forms of resistance develop, something new occurs, not precisely what was planned. The apparent aim of a gender interpellation even at the earliest stages may well eventuate in a fully different aim being realized. That "turning" of the aim happens in the midst of enactment: we find ourselves doing something else, doing ourselves in a way that was not exactly what anyone had in mind for us.

Although there are authoritative discourses on gender—the law, medicine, and psychiatry, to name a few—and they seek to launch and sustain human life within discrete gendered terms, they do not always succeed in containing the effects of those discourses of gender they bring into play. Moreover, it turns out that there can be no reproduction of gendered norms without the bodily enactment of those norms, and when that field of norms breaks open, even if provisionally, we see that the animating aims of a regulatory discourse, as it is enacted bodily, give rise to consequences that are not always foreseen, making room for ways of living gender that challenge prevailing norms of recognition. Thus we can plainly see the emergence of transgender, genderqueer, butch, femme, and hyperbolic or dissident modes of masculinity and femininity, and even zones of gendered life that are opposed to all categorical distinctions such as these. Some years ago, I tried to locate in gender performativity a form of inadvertent agency, one that was certainly not outside of all culture, power, and discourse, but that emerged, importantly, from within its terms, its unforeseeable deviations, establishing cultural possibilities that confounded the sovereign aims of all those institutional regimes, including parenting structures, that seek to know and normalize gender in advance.

So, first and foremost, to say that gender is performative is to say that it is a certain kind of enactment; the "appearance" of gender is often mistaken as a sign of its internal or inherent truth; gender is prompted by obligatory norms that demand that we become one gender or the other (usually within a strictly binary frame); the reproduction of gender is thus always a negotiation with power; and finally, there is no gender without this reproduction of norms that in the course of its repeated enactments risks undoing or redoing the norms in unexpected ways, opening up the possibility of remaking gendered reality along new lines. The political aspiration of this analysis, perhaps its normative aim, is to let the lives of gender and sexual minorities become more possible and more livable, for bodies that are gender nonconforming as well as those that conform too well (and at a high cost) to be able to breathe and move more freely in public and private spaces, as well as all those zones that cross and confound those two. Of course, the theory of gender performativity that I formulated never prescribed which gender performances were right, or more subversive, and which were wrong, and reactionary, even when it was clear that I valued the breakthrough of certain kinds of gender performances into public space, free of police brutality, harassment, criminalization, and pathologization. The point was precisely to relax the coercive hold of norms on gendered life—which is not the same as transcending or abolishing all norms—for the purposes of living a more livable life. This last is a normative view not in the sense that it is a form of normality, but only in the sense that it represents a view of the world as it should be. Indeed, the world as it should be would have to safeguard breaks with normality, and offer support and affirmation for those who make those breaks.

Perhaps it is possible to see how precarity has always been in this picture, since gender performativity was a theory and a practice, one might say, that opposed the unlivable conditions in which gender and sexual minorities live (and sometimes also those gender majorities who "passed" as normative at very high psychic and somatic costs). "Precarity" designates that politically induced condition in which certain populations suffer from failing social and economic networks of support more than others, and become differentially exposed to injury, violence, and death. As I mentioned earlier, precarity is thus the differential distribution of precariousness. Populations that are differentially exposed suffer heightened risk of disease, poverty, starvation, displacement, and vulnerability to violence without adequate protection or redress. Precarity also characterizes that politically induced condition of maximized vulnerability and exposure for populations exposed to arbitrary state violence, to street or domestic violence, or other forms not enacted by states but for which the judicial instruments of states fail to provide sufficient protection or redress. So by using the term precarity, we may be referring to populations who starve or who are near starvation, those whose food sources arrive one day but not the next or are carefully rationed—as we see when the state of Israel decides how much food Palestinians in Gaza need to survive—or any number of global examples where housing is temporary or lost. We might also be talking about transgendered sex workers who have to defend themselves against street violence and police harassment. And sometimes these are the same groups, and sometimes they are different. But when they are part of the same population, they are linked by their sudden or protracted subjection to precarity, even if they do not want to acknowledge this bond.

In this way, precarity is, perhaps obviously, directly linked with gender norms, since we know that those who do not live their genders in intelligible ways are at heightened risk for harassment, pathologization, and violence. Gender norms have everything to do with how and in what way we can appear in public space, how and in what way the public and private are distinguished, and how that distinction is instrumentalized in the service of sexual politics. By asking who will be criminalized on the basis of their public appearance, I mean, who will be treated as a criminal, and produced as a criminal (which is not always the same as being named a criminal by a code of law that discriminates against manifestations of certain gender norms or certain sexual practices); who will fail to be protected by the law or, more specifically, the police, on the street, or on the job, or in the home—in legal codes or religious institutions? Who will become the object of police violence? Whose claims of injury will be refused, and who will be stigmatized and disenfranchised at the same time that they become the object of fascination and consumer pleasure? Who will have medical benefits before the law? Whose intimate and kinship relations will be recognized before the law or criminalized by the law, or who will find themselves within a space of traveling fifteen miles a new subject of rights or a criminal? The legal status of many relationships (conjugal, parental) shifts quite radically depending on which jurisdiction one is under, whether the court is religious or secular, and whether or not the tension between competing legal codes happens to be resolved at the moment one appears.

The question of recognition is an important one, for if we say that we believe all human subjects deserve equal recognition, we presume that all human subjects are equally recognizable. But what if the highly regulated field of appearance does not admit everyone, requiring zones where many are expected not to appear or are legally proscribed from doing so? Why is that field regulated in such a way that only certain kinds of beings can appear as recognizable subjects, and others cannot? Indeed, the compulsory demand to appear in one way rather than another functions as a precondition of appearing at all. And this means that embodying the norm or norms by which one gains recognizable status is a way of ratifying and reproducing certain norms of recognition over others, and so constraining the field of the recognizable.

This is surely one question posed by the animal rights movements, since why is it that only human subjects are recognized and not nonhuman living beings? Does the act by which humans achieve recognition implicitly pick out only those features of the human that could arguably be separated off from the rest of animal life? The conceit of this form of recognition founders on itself, for would such a distinctly human creature actually be recognizable if it were somehow separated from its creaturely existence? What would it look like? That question is linked with, and confounded by, a related one: Which humans count as the human? Which humans are eligible for recognition within the sphere of appearance, and which are not? What racist norms, for instance, operate to distinguish among those who can be recognized as human and those who cannot?—questions made all the more relevant when historically entrenched forms of racism rely on bestial constructions of blackness. The very fact that I can ask which humans are recognized as human and which are not means that there is a distinct field of the human that remains unrecognizable, according to dominant norms, but which is obviously recognizable within the epistemic field opened up by counterhegemonic forms of knowing. On the one hand, this is a clear contradiction: one group of humans is recognized as human and another group of humans, ones who are human, is not recognized as human. Perhaps the one who writes such a sentence sees that both groups are equally human, and another group does not. That other group still holds to some criterion about what constitutes the human, even if it is not one that has become explicitly thematized. If that second group wishes to argue in favor of its version of the human, it will be caught in a bind, since the claim that one group is human, even paradigmatically human, is meant to introduce a criterion by which anyone who seems to be human can be judged to be so. And the criterion set forth by the second group will fail to secure the kind of agreement it requires in order to be true. That criterion presumes the realm of the nonhuman human, and depends on it to be differentiated from the paradigm of the human it seeks to defend. This is the kind of thinking that drives people mad, of course, and that seems right. One has to use reasonable language in the wrong way, and even commit errors of logic in order precisely to bring out this rupture induced by norms of recognition that constantly differentiate among those who ought to be recognized and those who ought not to be recognized. We are pitched into cruel and curious quandaries: a human not recognized as human is no human, and so we should not refer to them as if they were. We can see this as a key formulation of explicit racism that displays its contradiction even as it imposes its norm. As much as we need to understand that norms of gender are relayed through psychosocial fantasies that are not first of our own making, we can see that norms of the human are formed by modes of power that seek to normalize certain versions of the human over others, either distinguishing among humans, or expanding the field of the nonhuman at will. To ask how these norms are installed and normalized is the beginning of the process of not taking the norm for granted, of not failing to ask how it has been installed and enacted, and at whose expense. For those effaced or demeaned through the norm they are expected to embody, the struggle becomes an embodied one for recognizability, a public insistence on existing and mattering. Thus, only through a critical approach to the norms of recognition can we begin to dismantle those more vicious forms of logic that uphold forms of racism and anthropocentrism. And only through an insistent form of appearing precisely when and where we are effaced does the sphere of appearance break and open in new ways.

A critical theory of this kind is constantly beset by a set of linguistic quandaries: What do we call those who do not and cannot appear as "subjects" within hegemonic discourse? One obvious response is to repose the question: What do the excluded call themselves? How do they appear, through what conventions, and with what effect on dominant discourses that work through taken-for-granted logical schemes? Although gender cannot function as the paradigm for all forms of existence that struggle against the normative construction of the human, it can offer us a point of departure for thinking about power, agency, and resistance. If we accept that there are sexual and gender norms that condition who will be recognizable and "legible" and who will not, we can begin to see how the "illegible" may form as a group, developing forms of becoming legible to one another, how they are exposed to differential forms of living gender violence, and how this common exposure can become the basis for resistance.

To understand, for instance, that they are misrecognized or remain unrecognizable precisely, it may be necessary to understand how they exist—and persist—at the limits of established norms for thinking, embodiment, and even personhood. Are there forms of sexuality for which there is no good vocabulary precisely because the powerful logics that determine how we think about desire, orientation, sexual acts, and pleasures do not allow them to become legible? Is there not a critical demand to rethink our existing vocabularies, or revalorize devalued names and forms of address precisely to open up the norms that limit not only what is thinkable, but the thinkability of gender nonconforming lives?

The performativity of gender presumes a field of appearance in which gender appears, and a scheme of recognizability within which gender shows up in the ways that it does; and since the field of appearance is regulated by norms of recognition that are themselves hierarchical and exclusionary, the performativity of gender is thus bound up with the differential ways in which subjects become eligible for recognition. Recognizing a gender depends fundamentally on whether there is a mode of presentation for that gender, a condition for its appearance; we can call this its media or its mode of presentation. As much as that is true, it is also true that gender can sometimes appear in ways that draw upon, rework, or even break with established conditions of appearance, breaking with existing norms or importing norms from unanticipated cultural legacies. Even as norms seem to determine which genders can appear and which cannot, they also fail to control the sphere of appearance, operating more like absent or fallible police than effective totalitarian powers. Further, if we think more carefully about recognition, we have to ask, is there a way to distinguish between full and partial recognition, and even a way to distinguish recognition from misrecognition? The latter proves quite important to consider given that recognizing a gender very often involves recognizing a certain bodily conformity with a norm, and norms are to a certain degree composed of ideals that are never fully inhabitable. So, in recognizing a gender, one recognizes the trajectory of a certain striving to inhabit a regulated ideal, one whose full embodiment would doubtless sacrifice some dimension of creaturely life. If any of us "become" a normative ideal once and for all, we have then overcome all striving, all inconsistency, all complexity, that is, lost some crucial dimension of what it is to be living. Hypernormative gender can kick some living creatures to the curb. But sometimes it is the "hyper" that works with and against that constitutive misfire with deliberation, tenacity, and pleasure, with a felt sense of rightness; it can be a way of creating new modes of transgendered living worthy of support. Yet, other times, there is a way of closing that gap so that the gender one feels oneself to be becomes the gender by which one is recognized, and that rightness is the precondition of livable life. The gender ideal is not a trap, but a desirable way of life, a way of embodying a sense of rightness that requires, and deserves, recognition.

Even if something called full embodiment and full recognition is something of a fantasy, one that threatens to lock us into a certain ideals that deprive us of the living character of our existences, is it possible to live well without any fantasy of that kind? A livable life can follow from a demand to live out the corporeal sense of gender, and so to escape from a restriction that does not allow that way of being to live freely in the world. To be radically deprived of recognition threatens the very possibility of existing and persisting.[3] To be a subject at all requires first finding one's way with certain norms that govern recognition, norms we never chose, and that found their way to us and enveloped us with their structuring and animating cultural power. And so, if we cannot find our way within the norms of gender or sexuality assigned to us, or can only find our way with great difficulty, we are exposed to what it means to be at the limits of recognizability: this situation can be, depending on the circumstance, both terrible and exhilarating. To exist at such a limit means that the very viability of one's life is called into question, what we might call the social ontological conditions of one's persistence. It also means that we can be at the threshold of developing the terms that allow us to live.

In some liberal discourses, subjects are thought of as the kind of beings who come before an existing law and ask for recognition within its terms. But what makes it possible to even come before the law (a Kafkan question, to be sure)? It would seem that one has to have access or standing, or that one has to be able to enter and to appear in some form. Preparing a defendant to stand trial is all about producing the subject whose bid for recognition stands a chance. This often means conforming to racial norms, or producing oneself as "postracial." The "law" is already working before the defendant enters into the courtroom; it takes the form of a regulatory structuring of the field of appearance that establishes who can be seen, heard, and recognized. The legal domain overlaps with the political field. We have only to think about the situation of undocumented workers who want work visas or citizenship, whose very bid to "become legal" is considered a criminal activity. Consulting a lawyer is itself an act that could expose the undocumented worker to arrest and deportation. Finding the right "conditions of appearance" is a complicated matter, since it is not just a matter of how the body presents itself before a court of law, but how one even gets a place in the queue that might possibly lead to a court appearance.

It may be that the rise of mass demonstrations in the last years by the undocumented is related to the motivations for demonstrations by those who have been abandoned by both political and economic processes (and the specific collusion between governments that sell off public services and neoliberal economics). The entrance of such populations into the sphere of appearance may well be making a set of claims about the right to be recognized and to be accorded a livable life, but it is also a way of laying claim to the public sphere, whether it is a radio broadcast, an assembly in the square, a march down the main streets of urban centers, or an uprising at the margins of the metropole.

It may well seem that I am petitioning for disenfranchised people to be accorded their proper place within an expanding conception of the human community. In some ways that is true, though that would not be a just summary of my effort here. If the normative trajectory of this project were to be restricted to such a claim, we would not be able to understand how the human is differentially produced, and at whose cost. Those who bear the cost, or who effectively "are" the cost of the human, its refuse or debris, are precisely those who sometimes find themselves unexpectedly allied with one another in a bid to persist and exercise forms of freedom that overcome narrow versions of individualism without being collapsed into compulsory forms of collectivism.

To think critically about how the norm of the human is constructed and maintained requires that we take up a position outside of its terms, not just in the name of the nonhuman or even the antihuman, but, rather, in a form of sociality and interdependence that is not reducible to human forms of life and that cannot be adequately addressed by any obligatory definition of human nature or the human individual. To speak about what is living in human life is already to admit that human ways of living are bound up with nonhuman modes of life. Indeed, the connection with nonhuman life is indispensable to what we call human life. In Hegelian terms: if the human cannot be the human without the inhuman, then the inhuman is not only essential to the human, but is installed as the essence of the human. This is one reason that racists are so hopelessly dependent on their own hatred of those whose humanity they are finally powerless to deny.

The point is not to simply invert the relations such that we all gather under the banner of the nonhuman or the inhuman. And it is certainly not to accept the status of the excluded as "bare life" with no capacity to gather or resist. Rather, we start perhaps by holding in the mind this merely apparent paradox together in a new thought of "human life" in which its component parts, "human" and "life," never fully coincide with one another. In other words, we will have to hold on to this term even though, as a term, it will on occasion seek to contain two terms that repel one another, or that work in divergent directions. Human life is never the entirety of life, can never name all the life processes on which it depends, and life can never be the singularly defining feature of the human—so whatever we might want to call human life will inevitably consist of a negotiation with this tension. Perhaps the human is the name we give to this very negotiation that emerges from being a living creature among creatures and in the midst of forms of living that exceed us.

It is my hypothesis that ways of avowing and showing certain forms of interdependency stand a chance of transforming the field of appearance itself. Ethically considered, there has to be a way to find and forge a set of bonds and alliances, to link interdependency to the principle of equal value, and to do this in a way that opposes those powers that differentially allocate recognizability, or that disrupts its taken-for-granted operation. For once life is understood as both equally valuable and interdependent, certain ethical formulations follow. In *Frames of War,* I suggested that even if my life is not destroyed in war, something of my life is destroyed in war, when other lives and living processes are destroyed in war.[4] How does this follow? Since other lives, understood as part of life that exceeds me, are a condition of who I am, my life can make no exclusive claim on life, and my own life is not every other life, and cannot be. In other words, to be alive is already to be connected with what is living not only beyond myself, but beyond my humanness, and no self and no human can live without this connection to a biological network of life that exceeds the domain of the human animal. The destruction of valuable built environments and sustaining infrastructure is the destruction of what ideally should organize and sustain life in ways that are livable. Running water would be an emphatic case in point. This is one reason why in opposing war one not only opposes the destruction of other human lives (although one does), but the poisoning of the environment, and the more generalized assault on a living world. It is not just that the human who is dependent cannot survive on toxic soil, but that the human who toxifies the soil undermines the prospects for his or her own livability in a common world, where "one's own" prospects for living are invariably linked with everyone else's.

Only in the context of a living world does the human as an agentic creature emerge, one whose dependency on others and on living processes gives rise to the very capacity for action. Living and acting are bound together in such a way that the conditions that make it possible for anyone to live are part of the very object of political reflection and action. The ethical question, how ought I to live? or even the political question, how ought we to live together? depends upon an organization of life that makes it possible to entertain those questions meaningfully. So the question of what makes for a livable life is prior to the question of what kind of life I might live, which means that what some call the biopolitical conditions the normative questions we pose of life.

I take this to be an important critical rejoinder to political philosophers such as Hannah Arendt, who, in *The Human Condition*, quite emphatically distinguishes the private sphere as one of dependency and inaction from the public sphere as one of independent action. How are we to think about the passage from the private to the public, and do any of us leave the sphere of dependency "behind" even as we appear as self-standing actors within established public spheres? If action is defined as independent, implying a fundamental difference from dependency, then our self-understanding as actors is predicated upon a disavowal of those living and interdependent relations upon which our lives depend. If we are political actors who seek to establish the importance of ecology, the politics of the household, health care, housing, global food politics, and demilitarization, then it would seem that the idea of human and creaturely life that supports our efforts will be one that overcomes the schism between acting and interdependency. Only as creatures who recognize the conditions of interdependency that ensure our persistence and flourishing can any of us struggle for the realization of any of those important political goals during times in which the very social conditions of existence have come under economic and political assault.

The implications for political performativity seem important. If performativity implies agency, what are then the living and social conditions of agency? It cannot be that agency is a specific power of speech, and that the speech act is the model of the political action. That Arendtian presupposition from *The Human Condition* presumes that the body does not enter into the speech act, and that the speech act is understood as a mode of thinking and judging. The public sphere in which the speech act qualifies as the paradigmatic political action is one that has already, in her view, been separated from the private sphere, the domain of women, slaves, children, and those too old or infirm to work. In a sense, all those populations are associated with the bodily form of existence, one characterized by the "transience" of its work, and contrasted with true deeds, which include the making of cultural works and the spoken deed. The implicit distinction between body and mind in *The Human Condition* has garnered the critical attention of feminist theorists for some time.[5] Significantly, this view of the foreign, unskilled, feminized body that belongs to the private sphere is the condition of possibility for the speaking male citizen (who is presumably fed by someone and sheltered somewhere, and whose nourishment and shelter are tended to in some regular ways by some disenfranchised population or another).

To be fair, Arendt does remark in *On Revolution* that the revolution is embodied. Referring to "the poor who came streaming out into the street," she writes that something "irresistible" motivates them, and this "irresistibility, which we found so intimately connected with the original meaning of 'revolution,' was embodied." And yet, she immediately links this "element of irresistibility" with "the necessity which we ascribe to natural processes . . . because we experience necessity to the extent that we find ourselves, as organic bodies, subject to necessary and irresistible processes." When the poor come streaming into the streets, they act from necessity, from hunger and need, and they seek to "achieve such liberation [from life's necessities] . . . by means of violence." As a result, she tells us, "necessity invaded the political realm, the only realm where men can be truly free."[6] The political movement that is motivated by hunger is understood to be motivated by necessity and not freedom, and the form of liberation it seeks is not freedom, but an impossible and violent effort to be freed from the necessities of life. It would seem to follow that social movements of the poor are not seeking to relieve the poor of poverty, but of necessity, and that, as she clearly states, the violence between men for whom the necessities of life are already taken care of is "less terrifying" than the violence undertaken by the poor. In her view, "nothing, we might say today, could be more obsolete than to attempt to liberate mankind from poverty by political means."[7] Not only do we see an operative distinction between "liberation" and "freedom" that clearly implies that liberation movements operate with a less than "true" sense of freedom, but the political domain is once again adamantly distinguished from the domain of economic need. For Arendt, it would seem, those who act from necessity act from the body, but necessity can never be a form of freedom (the two are opposites), and freedom can only be achieved by those who are, well, not hungry. But what about the possibility that one might be hungry, angry, free, and reasoning, and that a political movement to overcome inequality in food distribution is a just and fair political movement? If the body remains at the level of necessity, then it would appear that no political account of freedom can be an embodied one.

Linda Zerilli has made an excellent argument that Arendt's reference to the body as a sphere of necessity is meant to mark the rhythmic patterns of transience, the fact that human artifacts come into the world and pass away, and this fact of mortality casts its shadow on both human forms of making (poeisis) and acting (praxis).[8] What we might understand as the relentless and repetitive mortality of the body cannot be addressed or relieved by human action. There is no "flight from embodied existence" understood as "necessity" without the loss of freedom itself. Freedom requires this reconciliation with necessity. This formulation makes good sense as long as "embodied action" is identified with "necessity," but if freedom is embodied, the formulation proves to be overbroad. To seek a form of human action capable of overcoming death is itself impossible and dangerous, taking us further away from a sense of the precariousness of life. In this perspective, the body imposes a principle of humility and a sense of the necessary limit of all human action.

However, if we approach this question from the point of view of the unequal demographic distribution of precarity, then we would have to ask: Whose lives are cut short more easily? Whose lives are plunged into a greater sense of transience and early mortality? How is that differential exposure to mortality managed? In other words, we are already within the political when we think about transience and mortality. That does not mean that in a just world, there would be no mortality! Not at all. It means only that a commitment to equality and justice would entail addressing at every institutional level the differential exposure to death and dying that currently characterizes the lives of subjugated peoples and the precarious, often as the result of systematic racism or forms of calculated abandonment. Ruth Gilmore's now famous description of racism makes the point most clearly: "Racism, specifically, is the state-sanctioned or extralegal production and exploitation of group-differentiated vulnerability to premature death."[9]

Despite these clear limitations, Arendt gives us an opening to understanding how assembly and gathering work to establish or reestablish the space of appearance, even the demonstrations under the name "Black Lives Matter." For even if we cannot accept that the mortality of the body is a purely prepolitical condition of life, we can still find some important ways of understanding the embodied character of plural human action in her writings. Perhaps one purpose here is to try to rethink these distinctions in Arendt, showing that the body or, rather, concerted bodily action—gathering, gesturing, standing still, all of the component parts of "assembly" that are not quickly assimilated to verbal speech—can signify principles of freedom and equality.

Although I criticize some dimensions of the body politics offered by Hannah Arendt,[10] I want to draw attention to her text, "The Decline of the Nation-State and the End of the Rights of Man," that bears on the question of the rights of those without rights.[11] Arendt's assertion that even the stateless have the "the right to have rights" is itself a kind of performative exercise, as has been ably argued by Bonnie Honig and others; Arendt is establishing through her very claim the right to have rights, and there is no ground for this claim outside of the claim itself. And though sometimes that claim is understood as purely linguistic, it is clear that the claim is enacted through bodily movement, assembly, action, and resistance. In 2006, undocumented Mexican workers laid claim to their rights through singing the American anthem in Spanish in public; they laid claim to that right in and by the vocalization itself. And those who fought against the expulsion of the Roma—the gypsies—from France spoke not only for the Roma, but against the arbitrary and violent power of a state to expel into statelessness a segment of its population. Similarly, we can say that state authorization for the police to arrest and deport veiled women in France is another example of a discriminatory action that targets a minority, and that clearly denies their rights to appear in public as they will. French feminists who call themselves universalists have supported the law that would empower police to arrest, detain, fine, and deport women wearing a face veil on the streets of France. What sort of politics is this that recruits the police function of the state to monitor and restrict women from religious minorities in the public sphere? Why would the same universalists who openly affirm the rights of transgendered people to appear freely in public without police harassment at the same time support police detentions of Muslim women who wear religious clothing in public? Those who supported such a ban argued in the name of a universalist feminism, claiming that the veil offends the sensibilities of universalism.[12] So what kind of universalism is it that is grounded in a very specific secular tradition and that fails to honor the rights of religious minorities to follow codes of sartorial conduct? Even if one stayed within the problematic framework of that universalism, it would be difficult to come up with a coherent and noncontradictory criterion for why transgendered people should be protected against police violence and given every right to appear in public while Muslim women, but neither Christian nor Jewish women who may be engaged in wearing religious insignias, are to be deprived of the right to appear in public in ways that signify their religious affiliation and belonging. If rights can be universalized only for those who abide by secular norms, or who belong to religions that are deemed eligible for protection under the law, then surely the "universal" has become emptied of meaning or, worse, has become an instrument of discrimination, racism, and exclusion. If the right to appear is to be honored "universally" it would not be able to survive such an obvious and insupportable contradiction.

What we sometimes call a "right" to appear is tacitly supported by regulatory schemes that qualify only certain subjects as eligible to exercise that right. So no matter how "universal" the right to appear claims to be, its universalism is undercut by differential forms of power that qualify who can and cannot appear. For those who are considered "ineligible," the struggle to form alliances is paramount, and it involves a plural and performative positing of eligibility where it did not exist before. This kind of plural performativity does not simply seek to establish the place of those previously discounted and actively precarious within an existing sphere of appearance. Rather, it seeks to produce a rift within the sphere of appearance, exposing the contradiction by which its claim to universality is posited and nullified. There can be no entry into the sphere of appearance without a critique of the differential forms of power by which that sphere is constituted, and without a critical alliance formed among the discounted, the ineligible—the precarious—to establish new forms of appearance that seek to overcome that differential form of power. It may well be that every form of appearance is constituted by its "outside," but that is no reason not to continue the struggle. Indeed, that is only a reason to insist upon the struggle as ongoing.

SOMETIMES THERE ARE QUOTIDIAN acts that are very often at stake when we seek to understand performative politics in its struggle from and against precarity. As we know, not everyone can take for granted the power to walk on the street or into a bar without harassment. To walk on the street alone without police harassment is precisely not to walk with the company of others and whatever nonpolice forms of protection that supplies. And yet, when a transgendered person walks on the street in Ankara or into McDonald's in Baltimore,[13] there is a question of whether that right can be exercised by the individual alone. If the person is extraordinarily good at self-defense, perhaps it can; if it is in a cultural space where that is accepted, it surely can. But if and when it does become possible to walk unprotected and still be safe, for daily life itself to become possible without fear of violence, then it is surely because there are many who support that right even when it is exercised by one person alone. If the right is exercised and honored, it is because there are many there, exercising it as well, whether or not anyone else is on the scene. Each "I" brings the "we" along as he or she enters or exits that door, finding oneself in an unprotected enclosure or exposed out there on the street. We might say that there is a group, if not an alliance, walking there, too, whether or not they are anywhere to be seen. It is, of course, a singular person who walks there, who takes the risk of walking there, but it is also the social category that traverses that particular gait and walk, that singular movement in the world; and if there is an attack, it targets the individual and the social category at once. Perhaps we can still call "performative" both this exercise of gender and the embodied political claim to equality, the protection from violence, and the ability to move with and within this social category in public space. To walk is to say that this is a public space in which transgendered people walk, that this is a public space where people with various forms of clothing, no matter how they are gendered or what religion they signify, are free to move without threat of violence.

To be a participant in politics, to become part of concerted and collective action, one needs not only to make the claim for equality (equal rights, equal treatment), but to act and petition within the terms of equality, as an actor on equal standing with others. In that way the communities that assemble on the street start to enact another idea of equality, freedom, and justice than the one that they oppose. The "I" is thus at once a "we," without being fused into an impossible unity. To be a political actor is a function, a feature of acting on terms of equality with other humans—this important Arendtian formulation remains relevant to contemporary democratic struggles. Equality is a condition and character of political action itself at the same time that it is its goal. The exercise of freedom is something that does not come from you or from me, but from what is between us, from the bond we make at the moment in which we exercise freedom together, a bond without which there is no freedom at all.

In 2010, in Ankara, Turkey, I attended an international conference against homophobia and transphobia. This was an especially important event in Ankara, the capital of Turkey, where transgendered people are often served fines for appearing in public, are often beaten, sometimes by the police, and where murders of trans-gendered women in particular have taken place nearly once a month in recent years. If I offer you this example of Turkey, it is not to point out that Turkey is "behind"—something that the embassy representative from Denmark was quick to suggest to me, and which I declined to accept with equal speed. I assure you that there are equally brutal murders outside of Los Angeles and Detroit, in Wyoming and Louisiana, and harassment and beatings in Baltimore, as we know, and in Penn Station in New York City. Rather, what seemed exemplary about the alliances there is that several feminist organizations have worked with queer, gay/lesbian, and transgendered people against police violence, but also against militarism, nationalism, and the forms of masculinism by which they are supported. So on the street, after the conference, femi-nists lined up with the drag queens, genderqueers with human rights activists, and lipstick lesbians with their bisexual and het-erosexual friends; the march included secularists and Muslims. They chanted, "we will not be soldiers, and we will not kill." To oppose the police violence against trans people was thus to be openly against military violence and the nationalist escalation of militarism; it was also to oppose the military aggression against the Kurds and the failure to recognize their political claims, but also, to act in the memory of the Armenian genocide and against modes of disavowal on the part of states that continue their violence in other ways.

So in Turkey, feminists took to the streets with trans activists, but in many feminist circles, there continues to be resistance against making that kind of alliance. In France, for instance, some femi-nists who understand themselves as left, even materialist, have converged on the idea that transsexuality is a kind of pathology. Of course, there is a distinction between criminalizing queer and transgendered people who appear in public and pathologizing them as ill. The first position is a moral one, usually based on a spurious conception of public morality. To criminalize a population not only deprives them of protection against the police and other forms of public violence, but it seeks to undermine the political movement struggling for decriminalization and enfranchisement. To shift to the "illness" model—or, indeed, the "psychosis" model—is to recruit a pseudoscientific explanation for the purpose of discrediting certain embodied modes of existence that do no harm to others. Indeed, the pathologization model also works to undermine the political movement for enfranchisement, since the explanation implies that such sexual and gender minorities need "treatment" rather than rights. As a result, we should be wary of those efforts to grant transsexuals rights, as the Spanish government has done, at the same time that it adopts mental health standards that pathologize the very populations whose rights they defend. And in the United States and other countries dominated by the *Diagnostic and Statistical Manual of Mental Disorders* (the "DSM"), we should be equally wary of those stipulated modes of "transition" that require that trans people establish a pathological condition in order to be eligible for financial support for their transitions and legal recognition as trans or as whatever gender is desired.

If trans people must sometimes pass through "pathologization" as a way to realize the nonpathological character of their desire and to establish an embodied way of life that is livable, then the consequence in those cases is that the price of enfranchisement is living through pathologization. What kind of enfranchisement is this, and how might it be possible not to pay such a terrible price? The instruments we use become stronger the more we use them and the more often they achieve desired results. But desired results are not always the same as wider social and political effects. So it seems we need to think about the kind of claim that trans-sexuality is making, one that is linked to the right to appear in public, to exercise freedom of this kind, and that is implicitly linked with every other struggle to appear on the street without the threat of violence. In this sense, the freedom to appear is central to any democratic struggle, which means that a critique of the political forms of appearance, including forms of constraint and mediation through which any such freedom can appear, is crucial to understanding what that freedom can be, and what interventions are required.

Of course, all this still leaves unaddressed what it means to appear, and whether that right does not privilege the idea of bodily presence or what some would call the "metaphysics of presence." Does the media not select what can appear, and who can appear? And what about those who prefer not to appear, who engage in their democratic activism in another way? Sometimes political action is more effective when launched from the shadows or the margins, and that is one important point—for instance, the association of Palestinian Queers for Boycott, Divestment, and Sanctions has questioned the idea that queer activism demands full public exposure.[14] Surely every activist needs to negotiate how much exposure, and in what way, is necessary to achieve his or her political goals. It is a way of negotiating, we might say, between the need for protection and the demand to take a public risk. Sometimes that public face can be a set of words, and sometimes the bodies on the street need not speak to make their demand.

No one should be criminalized for his or her gender presentation, and no one should be threatened with a precarious life by
virtue of the performative character of one's gender presentation.
And yet, this claim that people ought to have protection against
harassment and intimidation, against criminalization when they
appear as whatever gender they are, does not in any way prescribe
whether or how to appear. Indeed, it is important not to impose U.S.-based norms of hypervisibility on those who have
other ways of making political community and of struggling for
their freedom. The point, rather, is to expose the injustice of criminalizing the presentation of gender. A criminal code that justifies
criminalization on the basis of gender presentation or appearance
is itself criminal and illegitimate. And if gender or sexual minorities are criminalized or pathologized for how they appear, how
they lay claim to public space, the language through which they
understand themselves, the means by which they express love or
desire, those with whom they openly ally, choose to be near, or
engage sexually, or how they exercise their bodily freedom, then
those acts of criminalization are themselves violent; and in that
sense, they are also unjust and criminal. To police gender is a criminal
act, an act by which the police become the criminal, and those who
are exposed to violence are without protection. To fail to prevent
violence against minority communities on the part of the state police is itself a criminal negligence, at which point the police commit
a crime, and minorities are left precarious on the street.

When we exercise the right to be the gender we are or when
we exercise the right to engage in sexual practices that cause injury to no one, then we are certainly exercising a certain freedom.
So even if one feels that one has not chosen one's sexuality or
gender, that it is given by nature or by some other external

authority, the situation remains the same: if one is to claim that sexuality as a right over and against a set of laws or codes that consider it criminal or dishonorable, then the claim itself is performative. This is one way of naming that exercise of the right precisely when there is no local law to protect that exercise. There may be, of course, a local community, and an international set of precedents, but that does not always protect the one who makes the claim locally, as you know. But what is, in my mind, most important is that one claims such a position in public, that one walks the streets as one does, that one finds employment and housing without discrimination, that one is protected from street violence and police torture.

Even when one chooses to be who one is, and who one "is" is conceived as nonchosen, one has made freedom part of that very social project. One does not begin as one's gender and then later decide how and when to enact it. The enactment, which starts prior to any action of the "I," is part of the very ontological mode of gender, and so it matters how and when and with what consequences that enactment takes place, because all that changes the very gender that one "is." So, it is not possible to separate the genders that we are and the sexualities that we engage in from the right that each of us has to assert those realities in public, freely, and with protection from violence. In a way, the sexuality does not precede the right; the exercise of sexuality is an exercise of the right to do precisely that. It is a social moment within our intimate lives, and one that lays claim to equality; it is not just gender and sexuality that are in some sense performative, but their political articulation and the claims made on their behalf.

We can then return to the question, what does it means to lay claim to rights when one has none? It means to lay claim to the very power that one is denied in order to expose and militate against that denial. Like those squatter movements in Buenos Aires in which those without homes move into buildings in order to establish the grounds to claim rights of residency,[15] sometimes it is not a question of first having power and then being able to act; sometimes it is a question of acting, and in the acting, laying claim to the power one requires. This is performativity as I understand it, and it is also a way of acting from and against precarity.

Precarity is the rubric that brings together women, queers, transgender people, the poor, the differently abled, and the stateless, but also religious and racial minorities: it is a social and economic condition, but not an identity (indeed, it cuts across these categories and produces potential alliances among those who do not recognize that they belong to one another). And I believe we witnessed it in the Occupy Wall Street demonstrations—no one is ever asked to produce an identity card before gaining access to such a demonstration. If you appear as a body on the street, you help to make the claim that emerges from that plural set of bodies, amassing and persisting there. Of course, that can only happen if you can appear, if the streets are accessible, and you yourself are not confined. We will return to this problem when we consider "freedom of assembly" in Chapter 5.

The question of how performativity links with precarity might be summed up in these more important questions: How does the unspeakable population speak and make its claims? What kind of disruption is this within the field of power? And how can such populations lay claim to what they require in order to persist? It is not only that we need to live in order to act, but that we have to act, and act politically, in order to secure the conditions of existence. Sometimes the norms of recognition bind us in ways that imperil our capacity to live: What if the gender that establishes the norms required in order for us to be recognizable also does violence to us, imperils our very survival? Then the very categories that appear to promise us life take our life away. The point is not to accept such a double bind, but to strive for modes of life in which performative acts struggle against precarity, a struggle that seeks to open a future in which we might live in new social modes of existence, sometimes on the critical edge of the recognizable and sometimes in the limelight of the dominant media—but in either case, or in the spectrum between, there is a collective acting without a preestablished collective subject; rather, the "we" is enacted by the assembly of bodies, plural, persisting, acting, and laying claim to a public sphere by which one has been abandoned.

PERHAPS THERE ARE MODALITIES of violence that we need to think about in order to understand the police functions in operation here. After all, those who insist that gender must always appear in one way or in one clothed version rather than another, who seek either to criminalize or to pathologize those who live their gender or their sexuality in nonnormative ways, are themselves acting as the police for the sphere of appearance whether or not they belong to any police force. As we know, it is sometimes the police force of the state that does violence to sexual and gendered minorities, and sometimes it is the police who fail to investigate, fail to prosecute as criminal the murder of transgendered women, or fail to prevent violence against transgendered members of the population.

In Arendtian terms, we can say that to be precluded from the space of appearance, to be precluded from being part of the plurality that brings the space of appearance into being, is to be deprived of the right to have rights. Plural and public action is the exercise of the right to place and belonging, and this exercise is the means by which the space of appearance is presupposed and brought into being.

Let me return to the notion of gender with which I began, both to draw upon Arendt and to clarify why I resist Arendt in some respects. If we say that gender is an exercise of freedom, we do not mean to say that everything that constitutes gender is freely chosen. We claim only that even those dimensions of gender that seem quite "hardwired"—either constitutive or acquired—ought to be possible to claim and exercise in a free way. I have, with this formulation, taken a certain distance from the Arendtian formulation. This exercise of freedom must be accorded the same equal treatment as any other exercise of freedom under the law. And, politically, we must call for the expansion of our conceptions of equality to include this form of embodied freedom. So what do we mean when we say that sexuality or gender is an exercise of freedom? To repeat: I do not mean to say that all of us choose our gender or our sexuality. We are surely formed by language and culture, by history, by the social struggles in which we participate, by forces both psychological and historical—in interaction, by the way that biological situations have their own history and efficacy. Indeed, we may well feel that what and how we desire are quite fixed, indelible or irreversible features of who we are. But regardless of whether we understand our gender or our sexuality as chosen or given, we each have a right to claim that gender and to claim that sexuality. And it makes a difference whether we can claim them at all. When we exercise the right to appear as the gender we already are—even when we feel we have no other choice—we are still exercising a certain freedom, but we are also doing something more.

When one freely exercises the right to be who one already is, and one asserts a social category for the purpose of describing that mode of being, then one is, in fact, making freedom part of that very social category, discursively changing the very ontology in question. It is not possible to separate the genders that we claim to be and the sexualities that we engage in from the right that any of us has to assert those realities in public or in private—or in the many thresholds that exist between the two—freely, that is, without threat of violence. When, long ago, I said that gender is performative, that meant that it is a certain kind of enactment, which means that one is not first one's gender and then later one decides how and when to enact it. The enactment is part of its very ontology, is a way of rethinking the ontological mode of gender, and so it matters how and when and with what consequences that enactment takes place, because all that changes the very gender that one "is."

We can understand that change, for instance, in the significant acts by which initial gender assignment is refused or revised. Language exercises a distinct performative effect on the body in the act of being named as this or that gender or another gender, as it does when one is referred to, from the start, when language is still inchoate, as a particular color or race or nationality or as disabled or poor. To find out that how one is regarded in any of these respects is summed up by a name that one did not know or choose, surrounded and infiltrated by discourse that acts in ways that one cannot possibly understand when it first starts acting on one. We can, and do, ask, "Am I that name?"[16] And sometimes we keep on asking it until we make a decision that we are or are not that name, or we try to find a better name for the life we wish to live, or we endeavor to live in the interstices among all the names.

How do we think about the force and effect of those names we are called before emerging into language as speaking beings, prior to any capacity for a speech act of our own? Does speech act upon us prior to our speaking, and if it did not act upon us, could we speak at all? And perhaps it is not simply a matter of sequence: Does speech continue to act upon us at the very moment in which we speak, so that we may well think we are acting, but we are also acted upon at that very same time?

Several years ago, Eve Sedgwick underscored that speech acts deviate from their aims, very often producing consequences that are altogether unintended, and oftentimes quite felicitous.[17] For instance, one could take a marriage vow, and this act could actually open up a zone of sexual life that takes place quite separately from marriage, often pursued under the radar. So, though marriage is understood to have the aim of organizing sexuality in monogamous and conjugal terms, it can establish a desired zone for a sexuality not exposed to public scrutiny and recognition. Sedgwick underscored how a speech act ("I pronounce you man and wife") could veer away from its apparent aims, and this "deviation" was one very important sense of the word queer, understood less as an identity than as a movement of thought, language, and action that moved in directions quite contrary to those explicitly recognized. As much as recognition seems to be a precondition of livable life, it can serve the purposes of scrutiny, surveillance, and normalization from which a queer escape may prove necessary precisely to achieve livability outside its terms.

In my earlier work, I was interested in how several discourses on gender seemed to create and circulate certain ideals of gender, generating those ideals but taking them to be natural essences or internal truths that were subsequently expressed in those ideals.

So the effect of a discourse—in this case, a set of gender ideals—was broadly misconstrued as the internal cause of one's desire and behavior, a core reality that was expressed in one's gestures and actions. That internal cause or core reality not only substituted for the social norm, but effectively masked and facilitated the operation of that norm. The formulation that "gender is performative" gave rise to two quite contrary interpretations: the first was that we radically choose our genders; the second was that we are utterly determined by gender norms. Those wildly divergent responses meant that something had not quite been articulated and grasped about the dual dimensions of any account of performativity. For if language acts upon us before we act, and continues acting in every instant in which we act, then we have to think about gender performativity first as "gender assignment"—all those ways in which we are, as it were, called a name, and gendered prior to understanding anything about how gender norms act upon and shape us, and prior to our capacity to reproduce those norms in ways that we might choose. Choice, in fact, comes late in this process of performativity. And then, following Sedgwick, we have to understand how deviations from those norms can and do take place, suggesting that something "queer" is at work at the heart of gender performativity, a queerness that is not so very different from the swerves taken by iterability in Derrida's account of the speech act as citational.

So let us assume, then, that performativity describes both the processes of being acted on and the conditions and possibilities for acting, and that we cannot understand its operation without both of these dimensions. That norms act upon us implies that we are susceptible to their action, vulnerable to a certain name-calling from the start. And this registers at a level that is prior to any possibility of volition. An understanding of gender assignment has to take up this field of an unwilled receptivity, susceptibility, and vulnerability, a way of being exposed to language prior to any possibility of forming or enacting a speech act. Norms such as these both require and institute certain forms of corporeal vulnerability without which their operation would not be thinkable. That is why we can, and do, describe the powerful citational force of gender norms as they are instituted and applied by medical, legal, and psychiatric institutions, and object to the effect they have on the formation and understanding of gender in pathological or criminal terms. And yet, this very domain of susceptibility, this condition of being affected, is also where something queer can happen, where the norm is refused or revised, or where new formulations of gender begin. Precisely because something inadvertent and unexpected can happen in this realm of "being affected," gender can emerge in ways that break with, or deviate from, mechanical patterns of repetition, resignifying and sometimes quite emphatically breaking those citational chains of gender normativity, making room for new forms of gendered life.

Gender performativity does not just characterize what we do, but how discourse and institutional power affect us, constraining and moving us in relation to what we come to call our "own" action. To understand that the names we are called are just as important to performativity as the names we call ourselves, we have to identify the conventions that operate in a broad array of gender-assigning strategies. Then we can see how the speech act affects and animates us in an embodied way—the field of susceptibility and affect is already a matter of a corporeal registration of some kind. Indeed, the embodiment implied by both gender and performance is one that is dependent on institutional structures and broader social worlds. We cannot talk about a body without knowing what supports that body, and what its relation to that support—or lack of support—might be. In this way, the body is less an entity than a living set of relations; the body cannot be fully dissociated from the infrastructural and environmental conditions of its living and acting. Its acting is always conditioned acting, which is one sense of the historical character of the body. Moreover, the dependency of human and other creatures on infrastructural support exposes a specific vulnerability that we have when we are unsupported, when those infrastructural conditions start to decompose, or when we find ourselves radically unsupported in conditions of precarity. Acting in the name of that support, without that support, is the paradox of plural performative action under conditions of precarity.[18]

Chapter 2

Bodies in Alliance and the Politics of the Street

In Chapter 1 I suggested that gender politics must make alliances with other populations broadly characterized as precarious. I pointed to certain forms of gender mobilization that seek to establish the rights of gender minorities or people of non-conforming genders to walk freely on the street, to maintain employment, and to resist harassment, pathologization, and criminalization. For the struggle for the rights of gender and sexual minorities to be a social justice struggle, that is, for it to be characterized as a radical democratic project, it is necessary to realize that we are but one population who has been and can be exposed to conditions of precarity and disenfranchisement. Further, the rights for which we struggle are plural rights, and that plurality is not circumscribed in advance by identity, that is, it is not a struggle to which only some identities can belong, and it is surely a struggle that seeks to expand what we mean when we say "we." Thus public exercise of gender, of the rights to gender, we might say, is already a social movement, one that depends more strongly on the links between people than on any notion of individualism. Its aim is to counter those military, disciplinary, and regulatory forces and regimes that would expose us to precarity, and though lives can be made precarious by virtue of any number of illnesses and natural disasters, it remains true that—as we saw so dramatically in New Orleans during and after Hurricane Katrina in 2005—how illnesses are handled or not handled by existing institutions, how natural disasters for certain areas are preventable for some populations and not for others, all lead to a demographic distribution of precarity. And this is true more broadly for the homeless and the poor, but also those who are exposed to ravaging insecurity and the sense of a damaged future as infrastructural conditions fall away or as neoliberalism replaces the sustaining institutions of social democracy with an entrepreneurial ethic that exhorts even the most powerless to take responsibility for their own lives without depending on anyone or anything else. It is as if under contemporary conditions, there is a war on the idea of interdependency, on what I elsewhere called the social network of hands that seek to minimize the unlivability of lives. So these plural sets of rights, rights we must see as collective and embodied, are not modes of affirming the kind of world any of us should be able to live in; rather, they emerge from an understanding that the condition of precarity is differentially distributed, and that the struggle against, or the resistance to, precarity has to be based on the demand that lives should be treated equally and that they should be equally livable. That also means that the form of resistance itself, that is, the way communities are organized to resist precarity, ideally exemplifies the very values for which those communities struggle. Alliances that have formed to exercise the rights of gender and sexual minorities must, in my view, form links, however difficult, with the diversity of their own population and all the links that implies with other populations subjected to conditions of induced precarity during our time. And this linking process, however difficult, is necessary because the population of gender and sexual minorities is itself diverse—a word that is not quite precise enough for what I want to say; this group draws from various class, racial, and religious backgrounds, crossing communities of language and cultural formation.

What I am calling alliance is not only a future social form; sometimes it is latent, or sometimes it actually is the structure of our own subject-formation, as when alliance happens within a single subject, when it is possible to say, "I am myself an alliance, or I ally with myself or my various cultural vicissitudes." That means only that the "I" in question refuses to background one minority status or lived site of precarity in favor of any other; it is a way of saying, "I am the complexity that I am, and this means that I am related to others in ways that are essential to any invocation of this 'I.'" Such a view, which implicates social relationality in the first-person pronoun, challenges us to grasp the insufficiency of identitarian ontologies for thinking about the problem of alliance. For the point is not that I am a collection of identities, but that I am already an assembly, even a general assembly, or an assemblage, as Jasbir Puar has adapted the term from Gilles Deleuze.[1] But perhaps what is most important are those forms of mobilization animated by a heightened awareness of the cross section of people at risk of losing employment and having their homes taken away by banks; the range of people who are differentially at risk for street harassment, criminalization, imprisonment, or pathologization; the specific racial and religious backgrounds of those people whose lives are targeted as dispensable by those who wage war. In my view, this perspective implies the need for a more generalized struggle against precarity, one that emerges from a felt sense of precarity, lived as slow death, a damaged sense of time, or unmanageable exposure to arbitrary loss, injury, or destitution—this is a felt sense that is at once singular and plural. The point is not to rally for modes of equality that would plunge us all into equally unlivable conditions. On the contrary, the point is to call for an equally livable life that is also enacted by those who make the call, and that requires the egalitarian distribution of public goods. The opposite of precarity is not security, but, rather, the struggle for an egalitarian social and political order in which a livable interdependency becomes possible—it would be at once the condition of our self-governing as a democracy, and its sustained form would be one of the obligatory aims of that very governance.

If I seem to have wandered from gender, I assure you that gender is still here. For one of the questions that any group representing the enfranchisement of women, sexual minorities, and gender minorities must consider is the following: What do we do when state governments or international organizations seek to champion our rights in order to explicitly conduct anti-immigration campaigns (as we have seen in France and in the Netherlands), or when states draw attention to their relatively progressive human rights record when it comes to women, lesbian and gay people, and transgendered people in order to deflect from an atrocious human rights record when it comes to those populations whose basic rights of self-determination, movement, and assembly are denied (as is the case in Israel's pinkwashing campaign, which deflects from the vast criminality of its occupation, land confiscation, and forced expulsion policies)? As much as we want our own rights to be recognized, we must oppose the deployment of that public recognition of our rights to deflect from and cover over the massive disenfranchisement of rights for others, including, in this instance, women, queers, and gender and sexual minorities who are living without the basic rights of citizenship in Palestine. I will return to this issue in Chapter 3, where I consider not just what it means to ally with one another, but what it means to live with one another. A politics of alliance, I will try to show, rests upon, and requires, an ethics of cohabitation. But for now, let me say that if the allocation of rights to one group is instrumentalized for the disenfranchisement of basic entitlements to another, then the group entitled is surely obligated to refuse the terms on which political and legal recognition and rights are being given. This does not mean that any of us give up existing rights, but only that we recognize that rights are only meaningful within a broader struggle for social justice, and that if rights are differentially distributed, then inequality is being instituted through the tactical deployment and justification for gay and lesbian rights. As a result, I propose we remember that the term queer does not designate identity, but alliance, and it is a good term to invoke as we make uneasy and unpredictable alliances in the struggle for social, political, and economic justice.

TIME AND AGAIN, mass demonstrations take place on the street, in the square, and though these are very often motivated by different political purposes, something similar nevertheless happens: bodies congregate, they move and speak together, and they lay claim to a certain space as public space. Now, it would be easier to say that these demonstrations or, indeed, these movements, are characterized by bodies that come together to make a claim in public space, but that formulation presumes that public space is given, that it is already public and recognized as such. We miss something of the point of these public demonstrations if we fail to see that the very public character of the space is being disputed, and even fought over, when these crowds gather. So though these movements have depended on the prior existence of pavement, street, and square, and have often enough gathered in squares such as Tahrir, whose political history is potent, it is equally true that the collective actions collect the space itself, gather the pavement, and animate and organize the architecture. As much as we must insist on there being material conditions for public assembly and public speech, we have also to ask how it is that assembly and speech reconfigure the materiality of public space and produce, or reproduce, the public character of that material environment. And when crowds move outside the square, to the side street or the back alley, to the neighborhoods where streets are not yet paved, then something more happens.

At such a moment, politics is not defined as taking place exclusively in the public sphere, distinct from the private one, but it crosses those lines again and again, bringing attention to the way that politics is already in the home, or on the street, or in the neighborhood, or indeed in those virtual spaces that are equally unbound by the architecture of the house and the square. So when we think about what it means to assemble in a crowd, a growing crowd, and what it means to move through public space in a way that contests the distinction between public and private, we see some ways that bodies in their plurality lay claim to the public, find and produce the public through seizing and reconfiguring the matter of material environments; at the same time, those material environments are part of the action, and they themselves act when they become the support for action. In the same way, when trucks or tanks are rendered inoperative and suddenly speakers climb onto them to address the crowd, the military instrument itself becomes a support or platform for a nonmilitary resistance, if not a resistance to the military itself; at such moments, the material environment is actively reconfigured and refunctioned, to use the Brechtian term. And our ideas of action then need to be rethought.

In the first instance, no one mobilizes a claim to move and assemble freely without moving and assembling together with others. In the second instance, the square and the street are not only the material supports for action, but they themselves are part of any account of bodily public action we might propose. Human action depends upon all sorts of supports—it is always supported action. We know from disability studies that the capacity to move depends upon instruments and surfaces that make movement possible, and that bodily movement is supported and facilitated by nonhuman objects and their particular capacity for agency. In the case of public assemblies, we see quite clearly the struggle over what will be public space, but also an equally fundamental struggle over how bodies will be supported in the world—a struggle for employment and education, equitable food distribution, livable shelter, and freedom of movement and expression, to name a few.

Of course, this produces a quandary. We cannot act without supports, and yet we must struggle for the supports that allow us to act or, indeed, that are essential components of our action. It was the Roman idea of the public square that formed the background for Hannah Arendt's understanding of the rights of assembly and free speech, of action and the exercise of rights. Hannah Arendt surely had both the classical Greek polis and the Roman forum in mind when she claimed that all political action requires the "space of appearance." She writes, for instance, "the polis, properly speaking, is not the city-state in its physical location; it is the organization of the people as it arises out of acting and speaking together, and its true space lies between people living together for this purpose, no matter where they happen to be."[2] The "true" space then lies "between the people," which means that as much as any action takes place in a located somewhere, it also establishes a space that belongs properly to alliance itself. For Arendt, this alliance is not tied to its location. In fact, alliance brings about its own location, highly transposable. She writes, "action and speech create a space between the participants which can find its proper location almost anywhere and anytime."[3]

So how do we understand this highly, if not infinitely trans-posable, notion of political space? Whereas Arendt maintains that politics requires the space of appearance, she also claims that space brings politics about: "it is the space of appearance in the widest sense of the word, namely, the space where I appear to others as others appear to me, where men [sic] exist not merely like other living or inanimate things but make their appearance explicitly."[4] Something of what she says here is clearly true. Space and location are created through plural action. And yet, in her view, action, in its freedom and its power, has the exclusive capacity to create location. Such a view forgets or refuses that action is always supported and that it is invariably bodily, even, as I will argue, in its virtual forms. The material supports for action are not only part of action, but they are also what is being fought about, especially in those cases when the political struggle is about food, employment, mobility, and access to institutions. To rethink the space of appearance in order to understand the power and effect of public demonstrations for our time, we will need to consider more closely the bodily dimensions of action, what the body requires, and what the body can do,[5] especially when we must think about bodies together in a historical space that undergoes a historical transformation by virtue of their collective action: What holds them together there, and what are their conditions of persistence and of power in relation to their precarity and exposure?

I would like to think about this itinerary by which we travel from the space of appearance to the contemporary politics of the street. Even as I say this, I cannot hope to gather together all the forms of demonstration we have seen, some of which are episodic, some of which are part of ongoing and recurrent social and political movements, and some of which are revolutionary. I hope to think about what might gather together these gatherings, these public demonstrations. During the winter of 2011, they included demonstrations against tyrannical regimes in North Africa and the Middle East, but also against the escalating precaritization of working peoples in Europe and the Southern Hemisphere, as well as the struggles for public education throughout the United States and Europe and, most recently, in Chile, and struggles to make the street safe for women and for gender and sexual minorities, including trans people, whose public appearance is too often punishable by legal and illegal violence. In public assemblies by trans and queer people, the claim is often made that the streets must be made safe from the police who are complicit in criminality; especially on those occasions when the police support criminal regimes or when, for instance, the police commit the very crimes against sexual and gender minorities that they are supposed to prevent. Demonstrations are one of the few ways that police power is overcome, especially when those assemblies become at once too large and too mobile, too condensed and too diffuse, to be contained by police power and when they have the resources to regenerate themselves on the spot.

Perhaps these are anarchist moments or anarchist passages, when the legitimacy of a regime or its laws is called into question, but when no new legal regimen has yet arrived to take its place. This time of the interval is one in which the assembled bodies articulate a new time and space for the popular will, not a single identical will, not a unitary will, but one that is characterized as an alliance of distinct and adjacent bodies whose action and whose inaction demand a different future. Together they exercise the performative power to lay claim to the public in a way that is not yet codified into law and that can never be fully codified into law. And this performativity is not only speech, but the demands of bodily action, gesture, movement, congregation, persistence, and exposure to possible violence. How do we understand this acting together that opens up time and space outside and against the established architecture and temporality of the regime, one that lays claim to materiality, leans into its supports, and draws from its material and technical dimensions to rework their functions? Such actions reconfigure what will be public and what will be the space of politics.

I push against Hannah Arendt even as I draw upon her resources to clarify my own position. Her work supports my action here, but I also refuse it in some ways. Arendt's view is confounded by its own gender politics, relying as it does on a distinction between the public and private domains that leaves the sphere of politics to men and reproductive labor to women. If there is a body in the public sphere, it is presumptively masculine and unsupported, presumptively free to create, but not itself created. And the body in the private sphere is female, ageing, foreign, or childish, and always prepolitical. Although she was, as we know from the important work of Adriana Cavarero, a philosopher of natality,[6] Arendt understood this capacity to bring something into being as a function of political speech and action. Indeed, when male citizens enter into the public square to debate questions of justice, revenge, war, and emancipation, they take the illuminated public square for granted as the architecturally bounded theater of their speech. And their speech becomes the paradigmatic form of action, physically cut off from the private domicile, which is itself shrouded in darkness and reproduced through activities that are not quite action in the proper and public senses. Men make the passage from that private darkness to that public light and, once illuminated, they speak, and their speech interrogates the principles of justice it articulates, becoming itself a form of critical inquiry and democratic participation. For Arendt, rethinking this classical scene within political modernity, speech is understood as the bodily and linguistic exercise of rights. Bodily and linguistic—how are we to reconceive these terms and their intertwining here against and beyond that presumption of a gendered division of labor?

For Arendt, political action takes place on the condition that the body appear. I appear to others, and they appear to me, which means that some space between us allows each to appear. One might expect that we appear within a space or that we are supported by a material organization of space. But that is not her argument. The sphere of appearance is not simple, since it seems to arise only on the condition of a certain intersubjective facing off. We are not simply visual phenomena for each other—our voices must be registered, and so we must be heard; rather, who we are, bodily, is already a way of being "for" the other, appearing in ways that we can neither see nor hear; that is, we are made available, bodily, for another whose perspective we can neither fully anticipate nor control. In this way, I am, as a body, not only for myself, not even primarily for myself, but I find myself, if I find myself at all, constituted and dispossessed by the perspective of others. So, for political action, I must appear to others in ways I cannot know, and in this way, my body is established by perspectives that I cannot inhabit but that, surely, inhabit me. This is an important point because it is not the case that the body only establishes my own perspective; it is also what displaces that perspective and makes that displacement into a necessity. This happens most clearly when we think about bodies that act together. No one body establishes the space of appearance, but this action, this performative exercise, happens only "between" bodies, in a space that constitutes the gap between my own body and another's. In this way, my body does not act alone when it acts politically. Indeed, the action emerges from the "between," a spatial figure for a relation that both binds and differentiates.

It is both problematic and interesting that, for Arendt, the space of appearance is not only an architectural given: "the space of appearance comes into being," she writes, "wherever men are together in the manner of speech and action, and therefore predates and precedes all formal constitution of the public realm and the various forms of government, that is, the various forms in which the public realm may be organized."[7] In other words, this space of appearance is not a location that can be separated from the plural action that brings it about; it is not there outside of the action that invokes and constitutes it. And yet, if we are to accept this view, we have to understand how the plurality that acts is itself constituted. How does a plurality form, and what material supports are necessary for that formation? Who enters this plurality, and who does not, and how are such matters decided?

How do we describe the action and the status of those beings disaggregated from the plural? What political language do we have in reserve for describing that exclusion and the forms of resistance that crack open the sphere of appearance as it is currently delimited? Are those who live on the outside of the sphere of appearance the deanimated "givens" of political life? Are they mere life or bare life? Are we to say that those who are excluded are simply unreal, disappeared, or that they have no being at all—shall they be cast off, theoretically, as the socially dead and the merely spectral? If we do that, we not only adopt the position of a particular regime of appearance, but ratify that perspective, even if our wish is to call it into question. Do such formulations describe a state of having been made destitute by existing political arrangements, or is that destitution unwittingly ratified by a theory that adopts the perspective of those who regulate and police the sphere of appearance itself?

At stake is the question of whether the destitute are outside of politics and power or are in fact living out a specific form of political destitution along with specific forms of political agency and resistance that expose the policing of the boundaries of the sphere of appearance itself. If we claim that the destitute are outside of the sphere of politics—reduced to depoliticized forms of being—then we implicitly accept as right the dominant ways of establishing the limits of the political. In some ways, this follows from the Arendtian position that adopts the internal point of view of the Greek polis on what politics should be, who should gain entry into the public square, and who should remain in the private sphere. Such a view disregards and devalues those forms of political agency that emerge precisely in those domains deemed prepolitical or extrapolitical and that break into the sphere of appearance as from the outside, as its outside, confounding the distinction between inside and outside. For in revolutionary or insurrectionary moments, we are no longer sure what operates as the space of politics, just as we are often unsure about exactly in what time we are living, since the established regimes of both space and time are upended in ways that expose their violence and their contingent limits. We see this, as mentioned earlier, when undocumented workers gather in the city of Los Angeles to claim their rights of assembly and of citizenship without being citizens, without having any legal right to do so. Their labor is supposed to remain necessary and shrouded from view, and so when these laboring bodies emerge on the street, acting like citizens, they make a mimetic claim to citizenship that alters not only how they appear, but how the sphere of appearance works. Indeed, the sphere of appearance is both mobilized and disabled when an exploited and laboring class emerges on the street to announce itself and express its opposition to being the unseen condition of what appears as political.

The impetus for Giorgio Agamben's notion of "bare life"[8] derives from this very conception of the polis in Arendt's political philosophy and, I would suggest, runs the risk of this very problem: if we seek to take account of exclusion itself as a political problem, as part of politics itself, then it will not do to say that once excluded, those beings lack appearance or "reality" in political terms, that they have no social or political standing or are cast out and reduced to mere being (forms of givenness precluded from the sphere of action). Nothing so metaphysically extravagant has to happen if we agree that one reason the sphere of the political cannot be defined by the classic conception of the polis is that we are then deprived of having and using a language for those forms of agency and resistance undertaken by the dispossessed. Those who find themselves in positions of radical exposure to violence, without basic political protections by forms of law, are not for that reason outside the political or deprived of all forms of agency. Of course,

we need a language to describe that status of unacceptable exposure, but we have to be careful that the language we use does not
further deprive such populations of all forms of agency and resistance, all ways of caring for one another or establishing networks
of support.

Although Agamben borrows from Foucault to articulate a
conception of the biopolitical, the thesis of "bare life" remains
untouched by that conception. As a result, we cannot within that
vocabulary describe the modes of agency and action undertaken
by the stateless, the occupied, and the disenfranchised, since even
the life stripped of rights is still within the sphere of the political
and is thus not reduced to mere being, but is, more often than not,
angered, indignant, rising up, and resisting. To be outside established and legitimate political structures is still to be saturated in
power relations, and this saturation is the point of departure for a
theory of the political that includes dominant and subjugated
forms, modes of inclusion and legitimation as well as modes of
delegitimation and effacement.

Luckily, I think Arendt did not consistently follow this model
from *The Human Condition,* which is why, for instance, in the early
1960s, she turned again to the fate of refugees and the stateless,
and came to assert in a new way the right to have rights.[9] The right
to have rights is one that depends on no existing particular political organization for its legitimacy. Like the space of appearance,
the right to have rights predates and precedes any political institution that might codify or seek to guarantee that right; at the
same time, it is derived from no natural set of laws. The right comes
into being when it is exercised, and exercised by those who act in
concert, in alliance. Those who are excluded from existing poli-
ties, who belong to no nation-state or other contemporary state

formation, may be deemed "unreal" only by those who seek to monopolize the terms of reality. And yet, even after the public sphere has been defined through their exclusion, they act. Whether they are abandoned to precarity or left to die through systematic negligence, concerted action still emerges from their acting together. And this is what we see, for instance, when undocumented workers amass on the street without the legal right to do so; when squatters lay claim to buildings in Argentina as a way of exercising the right to livable shelter; when populations lay claim to a public square that has belonged to the military; when refugees take part in collective uprisings demanding shelter, food, and rights of sanctuary; when populations amass, without the protection of the law and without permits to demonstrate, to bring down an unjust or criminal regime of law or to protest austerity measures that destroy the possibility of employment and education for many. Or when those whose public appearance is itself criminal— transgendered people in Turkey or women who wear the veil in France—appear in order to contest that criminal status and assert the right to appear.

The French law that prohibits "ostentatious" religious display in public as well as the hiding of the face seeks to establish a public sphere where clothing remains a signifier of secularism and the exposure of the face becomes a public norm. The prohibition against hiding the face serves a certain version of the right to appear, understood as the right for women to appear unveiled. At the same time, it denies the right to appear for that very group of women, requiring them to defy religious norms in favor of public ones. That required act of religious disaffiliation becomes obligatory when the public sphere is understood as one that overcomes or negates religious forms of belonging. The notion, prevalent in

French debate, that women who wear the veil cannot possibly do so from any sense of choice operates in the debate to veil, as it were, the blatant acts of discrimination against religious minorities that the law enacts. For one choice that is clearly made among those who wear the veil is not to comply with those forms of compulsory disaffiliation that condition the entrance to the public sphere. Here as elsewhere, the sphere of appearance is highly regulated. That these women be clothed in some ways rather than others constitutes a sartorial politics of the public sphere, but so too does compulsory "unveiling," itself a sign of belonging first to the public and only secondarily, or privately, to the religious community. This is especially pronounced in relation to Muslim women whose affiliations to various versions of public, secular, and religious domains may well be coterminous and overlapping. And it shows quite clearly that what is called "the public sphere" in such cases is built up through constitutive exclusions and compulsory forms of disavowal. Paradoxically, the act of conforming to a law that requires unveiling is the means by which a certainly highly compromised, even violent, "freedom to appear" is established.

Indeed, in the public demonstrations that often follow from acts of public mourning—as often occurred in Syria before half of its population became refugees, where crowds of mourners became targets of military destruction—we can see how the existing public space is seized by those who have no existing right to gather there, who emerge from zones of disappearance to become bodies exposed to violence and death in the course of gathering and persisting publicly as they do. Indeed, it is their right to gather, free of intimidation and the threat of violence, that is systematically attacked by the police, the army, hired gangs, or mercenaries. To attack those bodies is to attack the right itself, since when those bodies appear and act, they are exercising a right outside, against, and in the face of the regime.

Although the bodies on the street are vocalizing their opposition to the legitimacy of the state, they are also, by virtue of occupying and persisting in that space without protection, posing their challenge in corporeal terms, which means that when the body "speaks" politically, it is not only in vocal or written language. The persistence of the body in its exposure calls that legitimacy into question and does so precisely through a specific performativity of the body.[10] Both action and gesture signify and speak, both as action and claim; the one is not finally extricable from the other. Where the legitimacy of the state is brought into question precisely by that way of appearing in public, the body itself exercises a right that is no right; in other words, it exercises a right that is being actively contested and destroyed by military force and that, in its resistance to force, articulates its way of living, showing both its precarity and its right to persist. This right is codified nowhere. It is not granted from elsewhere or by existing law, even if it sometimes finds support precisely there. It is, in fact, the right to have rights, not as natural law or metaphysical stipulation, but as the persistence of the body against those forces that seek its debilitation or eradication. This persistence requires breaking into the established regime of space with a set of material supports both mobilized and mobilizing.

Just to be clear: I am not referring to a vitalism or a right to life as such. Rather, I am suggesting that political claims are made by bodies as they appear and act, as they refuse and as they persist under conditions in which that fact alone threatens the state with delegitimation. As much as bodies are exposed to political powers, they are also responsive to having been exposed, except in those

cases when the very conditions for responsiveness have been decimated. Although I do not doubt at all that it is possible to murder
the capacity for responsiveness in another person, I would caution
against taking that figure of full decimation as a way of describing
the struggle of the dispossessed. Although it is always possible to
err in the other direction, claiming that wherever there is power,
there is resistance, it would be a mistake to refuse the possibility
that power does not always work according to its aims, and that
visceral forms of rejection break out in consequential collective
forms. In those instances, bodies are themselves vectors of power
where the directionality of force can be reversed; they are embodied interpretations, engaging in allied action, to counter force
with another kind and quality of force. On the one hand, these
bodies are productive and performative. On the other hand, they
can persist and act only when they are supported, by environments,
by nutrition, by work, by modes of sociality and belonging. And
when these supports fall away and precarity is exposed, they are
mobilized in another way, seizing upon the supports that exist in
order to make a claim that there can be no embodied life without
social and institutional support, without ongoing employment,
without networks of interdependency and care, without collective rights to shelter and mobility. Not only do they struggle for
the idea of social support and political enfranchisement, but their
struggle is its own social form. And so, in the most ideal instances,
an alliance begins to enact the social order it seeks to bring about
by establishing its own modes of sociability. And yet, that alliance
is not reducible to a collection of individuals, and it is, strictly
speaking, not individuals who act. Moreover, action in alliance
happens precisely between those who participate, and this is not
an ideal or empty space. That interval is the space of sociality and

of support, of being constituted in a sociality that is never reducible to one's own perspective and to being dependent on structures without which there is no durable and livable life.

Many of the massive demonstrations and modes of resistance we have seen in the last months not only produce a space of appearance; they seize upon an already established space permeated by existing power, seeking to sever the relations between the public space, the public square, and the existing regime. So the limits of the political are exposed and the link between the theater of legitimacy and public space is severed; that theater is no longer unproblematically housed in public space, since public space now occurs in the midst of another action, one that displaces the power that claims legitimacy precisely by taking over the field of its effects. Simply put, the bodies on the street redeploy the space of appearance in order to contest and negate the existing forms of political legitimacy—and just as they sometimes fill or take over public space, the material history of those structures also works on them, becoming part of their very action, remaking a history in the midst of its most concrete and sedimented artifices. These are subjugated and empowered actors who seek to wrest legitimacy from an existing state apparatus that depends upon the regulation of the public space of appearance for its theatrical self-constitution. In wresting that power, a new space is created, a new "between" of bodies, as it were, that lays claim to existing space through the action of a new alliance, and those bodies are seized and animated by those existing spaces in the very acts by which they reclaim and resignify their meanings.

Such a struggle intervenes in the spatial organization of power, which includes the allocation and restriction of spatial locations in which and by which any population may appear, which implies a spatial regulation of when and how the "popular will" may appear. This view of the spatial restriction and allocation of who may appear—in effect, of who may become a subject of appearance—suggests an operation of power that works through both foreclosure and differential allocation.

What, then, does it mean to appear within contemporary politics, and can we consider this question at all without some recourse to the media? If we consider what it is to appear, it follows that we appear to someone and that our appearance has to be registered by the senses, not only our own, but someone else's. If we appear, we must be seen, which means that our bodies must be viewed and their vocalized sounds must be heard: the body must enter the visual and audible field. But is this not, of necessity, a laboring body and a sexual body, as well as a body gendered and racialized in some form? Arendt's view clearly meets its limits here, for the body is itself divided into the one that appears publicly to speak and act and another one, sexual, laboring, feminine, foreign, and mute, that generally is relegated to the private and prepolitical sphere. Such a division of labor is precisely what is called into question when precarious lives assemble on the street in forms of alliance that must struggle to achieve a space of appearance. If some domain of bodily life operates as the sequestered or disavowed condition for the sphere of appearance, it becomes the structuring absence that governs and makes possible the public sphere.

If we are living organisms who speak and act, then we are clearly related to a vast continuum or network of living beings; we not only live among them, but our persistence as living organisms depends on that matrix of sustaining interdependent relations. And yet, our speaking and acting distinguishes us as something separate from other living beings. Indeed, we do not need to know what is distinctively human about political action, but only finally to see how the entrance of the disavowed body into the political sphere establishes at the same time the essential link between humans and other living beings. The private body thus conditions the public body not only in theories such as Arendt's, but also in political organizations of space that continue in many forms (and that are in some sense naturalized in her theory). And even though the public and private body are not utterly distinct (bodies in private sometimes "show" in public, and every publicly exposed body has its private moments), the bifurcation is crucial to maintaining the public and private distinction and its modes of disavowal and disenfranchisement.

Perhaps it is a kind of fantasy that one dimension of bodily life can and must remain out of sight, and yet another, fully distinct, appears in public. Is there no trace of the biological in the sphere of appearance? Could we not argue, with Bruno Latour and Isabelle Stengers, that negotiating the sphere of appearance is, in fact, a biological thing to do, one of the investigative capacities of the organism? After all, there is no way of navigating an environment or procuring food without appearing bodily in the world, and there is no escape from the vulnerability and mobility that appearing in the world implies, which explains forms of camouflage and self-protection in the animal world. In other words, is appearance not a necessarily morphological moment where the body risks appearance not only in order to speak and act, but to suffer and move, as well, to engage others bodies, to negotiate an environment on which one depends, to establish a social organization for the satisfaction of needs? Indeed, the body can appear and signify in ways that contest the way it speaks or even contest speaking as its paradigmatic instance. Could we still understand action, gesture, stillness, touch, and moving together if they were all reducible to the vocalization of thought through speech?

This act of public speaking, even within that problematic division of labor, depends upon a dimension of bodily life that is given, passive, opaque, and so excluded from the conventional definition of the political. Hence, we can ask: What regulation keeps the given or passive body from spilling over into the active body? Are these two different bodies, and if so, what politics is required to keep them apart? Are these two different dimensions of the same body, or are these, in fact, the effect of a certain regulation of bodily appearance that is actively contested by new social movements, struggles against sexual violence, for reproductive freedom, against precarity, for the freedom of mobility? Here we can see that a certain topographical or even architectural regulation of the body happens at the level of theory. Significantly, it is precisely this operation of power—the foreclosure and differential allocation of whether and how the body may appear—that is excluded from Arendt's explicit account of the political. Indeed, her explicit account of the political depends upon that very operation of power that it fails to consider as part of politics itself.

So what I accept from Arendt is the following: Freedom does not come from me or from you; it can and does happen as a relation between us, or, indeed, among us. So this is not a matter of finding the human dignity within each person, but rather of understanding the human as a relational and social being, one whose action depends upon equality and articulates the principle of equality. Indeed, there is no human, in her view, if there is no equality. No human can be human alone. And no human can be human without acting in concert with others and on conditions of equality. I would add the following: The claim of equality is not only spoken or written, but is made precisely when bodies appear together, or, rather, when, through their action, they bring the space of appearance into being. This space is a feature and effect of action, and it works, according to Arendt, only when relations of equality are maintained.

Of course, there are many reasons to be suspicious of idealized moments, but there are also reasons to be wary of any analysis that is fully guarded against idealization. There are two aspects of the revolutionary demonstrations in Tahrir Square that I would like to underscore. The first has to do with the way a certain sociability was established within the square, a division of labor that broke down gender difference, that involved rotating who would speak and who would clean the areas where people slept and ate, developing a work schedule for everyone to maintain the environment and to clean the toilets. In short, what some would call "horizontal relations" among the protestors formed easily and methodically, alliances struggling to embody equality, which included an equal division of labor between the sexes—these became part of the very resistance to the Mubarak regime and its entrenched hierarchies, including the extraordinary differentials of wealth between the military and corporate sponsors of the regime and the working people. So the social form of the resistance began to incorporate principles of equality that governed not only how and when people spoke and acted for the media and against the regime, but how people cared for their various quarters within the square, the beds on the pavement, the makeshift medical stations and bathrooms, the places where people ate, and the places where people were exposed to violence from the outside. We are not just talking about heroic actions that took enormous physical strength and the exercise of compelling political rhetoric. Sometimes the simple act of sleeping there, in the square, was the most eloquent political statement—and even must count as an action. These actions were all political in the simple sense that they were breaking down a conventional distinction between public and private in order to establish new relations of equality; in this sense, they were incorporating into the very social form of resistance the principles they were struggling to realize in broader political forms.

Second, when up against violent attack or extreme threats, many people in the first Egyptian revolution of 2009 chanted the word *silmiyya,* which comes from the root verb *salima,* which means "to be safe and sound," "unharmed," "unimpaired," "intact," and "secure"; but also "to be unobjectionable," "blameless," "faultless"; and yet also "to be certain," "established," "clearly proven."[11] The term comes from the noun *silm,* which means "peace," but also, interchangeably and significantly, "the religion of Islam." One variant of the term is *hubb as-silm,* which is Arabic for "pacifism." Most usually, the chanting of *silmiyya* comes across as a gentle exhortation: "peaceful, peaceful." Although the revolution was for the most part nonviolent, it was not necessarily led by a principled opposition to violence. Rather, the collective chant was a way of encouraging people to resist the mimetic pull of military aggression—and the aggression of the gangs—by keeping in mind the larger goal: radical democratic change. To be swept into a violent exchange of the moment was to lose the patience needed to realize the revolution. What interests me here is the chant, the way in which language worked not to incite an action, but to restrain one: a restraint in the name of an emerging community of equals whose primary way of doing politics would not be violence.

It is clear that every assembly and demonstration that produced a change in regime in Egypt relied on the media to produce a sense of the public square and the space of appearance. Any provisional example of "the public square" is located, and it is transposable; indeed, it seemed to be transposable from the start, though never completely. And of course, we cannot think of the transposability of those bodies in the square without the media. In some ways, the media images from Tunisia prepared the way for the initial media events in Tahrir, then those that followed in Yemen, Bahrain, Syria, and Libya, all of which took different trajectories and take them still. Many of the public demonstrations of these last years have not been directed against military dictatorships or tyrannical regimes, and many of them have produced new state formations or conditions of war that are surely as problematic as those they replaced. But in some of the demonstrations that followed upon these uprisings, especially those that took aim at forms of induced precarity, participants have explicitly opposed monopoly capitalism, neoliberalism, and the suppression of political rights, and done so in the name of those who are abandoned by neoliberal reforms that seek to dismantle forms of social democracy and socialism, eradicate jobs, expose populations to poverty, and undermine the basic rights to public education and housing.

The street scenes become politically potent only when and if we have a visual and audible version of the scene communicated in live or proximate time, so that the media does not merely report the scene, but is part of the scene and the action; indeed, the media is the scene or the space in its extended and replicable visual and audible dimensions. One way of stating this is simply that the media extends the scene visually and audibly and participates in the delimitation and transposability of the scene. Put differently, the media constitutes the scene in a time and place that includes and exceeds its local instantiation. Although the scene is surely and emphatically local, those who are elsewhere have the sense that they are getting some direct access through the images and sounds they receive. That is true, but they do not know how the editing takes place, which scene conveys and travels and which scenes remain obdurately outside the frame. When the scene travels, it is both there and here, and if it were not spanning both locations— indeed, multiple locations—it would not be the scene that it is. Its locality is not denied by the fact that the scene is communicated beyond itself and so constituted in global media; it depends on that mediation to take place as the event that it is. This means that the local must be recast outside itself in order to be established as local, and this means that it is only through globalizing media that the local can be established and that something can really happen there. Of course, many things do happen outside the frame of the camera or other digital media devices, and the media can just as easily im- plement censorship as oppose it. There are many local events that are never recorded and broadcast, and some important reasons why. But when the event travels and manages to summon and sustain global outrage and pressure, which includes the power to stop mar- kets or to sever diplomatic relations, then the local will have to be established time and again in a circuitry that exceeds the local at every instant.

And yet, there remains something localized that cannot and does not travel in that way; and the scene could not be the scene if we did not understand that some people are at risk, and the risk is run precisely by those bodies on the street. If they are trans- ported in one way, they are surely left in place in another, holding the camera or the cell phone, face-to-face with those they oppose, unprotected, injurable, injured, persistent if not insurgent. It mat- ters that those bodies carry cell phones, relaying messages and images, and so, when they are attacked, it is more often than not in some relation to the camera or the video recorder. It can be an effort to destroy the camera and its user, or it can be a spectacle for the media produced as a warning or a threat. Or it can be a way to stop any more organizing. Is the action of the body separable from its technology, and is the technology not helping to establish new forms of political action? And when censorship or violence is directed against those bodies, is it not also directed against their access to media, in order to establish hegemonic control over which images travel and which do not?

Of course, the dominant media is corporately owned, exercising its own kinds of censorship and incitement. And yet, it still seems important to affirm that the freedom of the media to broadcast from these sites is itself an exercise of freedom and so a mode of exercising rights, especially when it is rogue media, from the street, evading the censor, where the activation of the instrument is part of the bodily action itself. This is doubtless why both Hosni Mubarak and David Cameron, eight months apart, argued for the censorship of social media networks. At least in some instances, the media not only reports on social and political movements that are laying claim to freedom and justice in various ways; the media also is exercising one of those freedoms for which the social movement struggles. I do not mean by this claim to suggest that all media is involved in the struggle for political freedom and social justice (we know, of course, that it is not). Of course, it matters which global media does the reporting and how. My point is that sometimes private media devices become global precisely at the moment in which they overcome modes of censorship to report protests, and in that way they become part of the protest itself.

What bodies are doing on the street when they are demonstrating is linked fundamentally to what communication devices and technologies are doing when they "report" on what is happening in the street. These are different actions, but they both require the body. The one exercise of freedom is linked to the other, which means that both are ways of exercising rights and that, jointly, they bring a space of appearance into being and secure its transposability. Although some may wager that the exercise of rights now takes place quite at the expense of bodies on the street, claiming that Twitter and other virtual technologies have led to a disembodiment of the public sphere, I would disagree in part. We have to think about the importance of media that is "hand held" or cell phones that are "held high," producing a kind of countersurveillance of military and police action. The media requires those bodies on the street to have an event, even as those bodies on the street require the media to exist in a global arena. But under conditions in which those with cameras or Internet capacities are imprisoned or tortured or deported, the use of the technology effectively implicates the body. Not only must someone's hand tap and send, but someone's body is on the line if that tapping and sending gets traced. In other words, localization is hardly overcome through the use of media that potentially transmits globally. And if this conjuncture of street and media constitutes a very contemporary version of the public sphere, then bodies on the line have to be thought of as both there and here, now and then, transported and stationary, with very different political consequences following from those two modalities of space and time.

It matters when public squares are filled to the brim, when people eat and sleep there, sing and refuse to cede that space, as we saw in the first gatherings in Tahrir Square, and continue to see in other parts of the world. It matters, as well, that it is public educational buildings that have been seized in Athens, London, and Berkeley. At the Berkeley campus, buildings were seized, and trespassing fines were handed out in response. In some cases, students were accused of destroying private property. But these very allegations raised the question of whether the university is public or private. The stated aim of the protest—for the students to seize the building and sequester themselves there—was a way to gain a platform, indeed, a way to secure the material conditions for appearing in public. Such actions generally do not take place when effective platforms are already available. The students there, but also in the United Kingdom more recently, were seizing buildings as a way to lay claim to buildings that ought properly, now and in the future, to belong to public education. That doesn't mean that every time these buildings are seized it is justifiable, but let us be alert to what is at stake here: the symbolic meaning of seizing these buildings is that these buildings belong to the public, to public education, and it is precisely the access to public education that is being undermined by fee and tuition hikes and budget cuts. We should not be surprised that the protest took the form of seizing the buildings, performatively laying claim to public education, insisting on gaining literal access to the buildings of public education precisely at a historical moment in which that access is being shut down. In other words, no positive law justifies these actions that oppose the institutionalization of unjust or exclusionary forms of power. Can we then say that these actions are nevertheless an exercise of a right, a lawless exercise that takes place precisely when the law is wrong or the law has failed?

The body on the street persists, but also seeks to find the conditions of its own preservation. Invariably, those conditions are social ones, and demand a radical reorganization of social life for those who experience their existence as imperiled. If we are thinking well, and our thinking commits us to the preservation of life in some form, then the life to be preserved takes a bodily form. In turn, this means that the life of the body—its hunger, its need for shelter and protection from violence—becomes a major issue of politics. Even the most given or unchosen features of our lives are not simply given; they are given in history and in language, in vectors of power that none of us chose. Equally true is that a given property of the body or a set of defining characteristics depends upon the continuing persistence of the body. Those social categories we never chose traverse this given body in some ways rather than in others, and gender, for instance, names that traversal as well as its transformations. In this sense, those most urgent and largely involuntary dimensions of our lives, which include hunger and the need for shelter, medical care, and protection from violence, natural or humanly imposed, are crucial to politics. We cannot presume the enclosed and well-fed space of the polis, where all the material needs are somehow being taken care of elsewhere by beings whose gender, race, or status render them ineligible for public recognition. Rather, we have not only to bring the material urgencies of the body into the square, but to make those needs central to the demands of politics.

In my view, a shared condition of precarity situates our political lives, even as precarity is differentially distributed. And some of us, as Ruth Gilmore has made very clear, are disproportionately more disposed to injury and early death than others.[12] Racial difference can be tracked precisely by looking at statistics on infant mortality, for example. This means, in brief, that precarity is unequally distributed and that lives are not considered equally grievable or equally valuable. If, as Adriana Cavarero has argued, the exposure of our bodies in public space constitutes us fundamentally and establishes our thinking as social and embodied, vulnerable and passionate, then our thinking gets nowhere without the presupposition of that very corporeal interdependency and entwinement. The body is constituted through perspectives it cannot inhabit; someone else sees our face in a way that we cannot and hears our voice in a way that we cannot. We are in this sense—bodily—always over there, yet here, and this dispossession marks the sociality to which we belong. Even as located beings, we are always elsewhere, constituted in a sociality that exceeds us. This establishes our exposure and our precarity, the ways in which we depend on political and social institutions to persist.

IN THOSE DEMONSTRATIONS where people sing and speak, but also arrange for medical care and provide provisional social services, can we distinguish those vocalizations emanating from the body from those other expressions of material need and urgency? In those instances in which demonstrators were, after all, sleeping and eating in the public square, constructing toilets and various systems for sharing the space, they were not only refusing to disappear, refusing to go or stay home, and not only claiming the public domain for themselves—acting in concert on conditions of equality—but also maintaining themselves as persisting bodies with needs, desires, and requirements: Arendtian and counter-Arendtian, to be sure, since these bodies who were organizing their basic needs in public were also petitioning the world to register what was happening there, to make its support known, and in that way to enter into revolutionary action itself. The bodies acted in concert, but they also slept in public, and in both these modalities, they were both vulnerable and demanding, giving political and spatial organization to elementary bodily needs. In this way, they formed themselves into images to be projected to all who watched, petitioning us to receive and respond and so to enlist media coverage that would refuse to let the event be covered over or slip away. Sleeping on that pavement was not only a way to lay claim to the public, to contest the legitimacy of the state, but also, quite clearly, a way to put the body on the line in its insistence, obduracy, and precarity, overcoming the distinction between public and private for the time of revolution. In other words, it was only when those needs that are supposed to remain private came out into the day and night of the square, formed into image and discourse for the media, that it finally became possible to extend the space and time of the event with such tenacity as to bring the regime down. After all, the cameras never stopped; bodies were there and here; they never stopped speaking, not even in sleep, and so could not be silenced, sequestered, or denied— revolution sometimes happens because everyone refuses to go home, cleaving to the pavement as the site of their convergent and temporary cohabitation.

Chapter 3

Precarious Life and the Ethics of Cohabitation

I hope to address here ethical obligations that are global in character and that emerge both at a distance and within relations of proximity. The two questions that concern me are at first quite different from one another. The first is whether any of us have the capacity or inclination to respond ethically to suffering at a distance, and what makes that ethical encounter possible when it does take place. The second is what it means for our ethical obligations when we are up against another person or group, find ourselves invariably joined to those we never chose, and must respond to solicitations in languages we may not understand or even wish to understand. This happens, for instance, at the border of several contested states, but also in various moments of geographical proximity—what we might call "up againstness"—the result of populations living in conditions of unwilled adjacency due to forced emigration or the redrawing of the boundaries of a nation-state. Of course, presumptions about farness and nearness are already there in most of the accounts of ethics that we know. There are communitarians who do not mind the local, provisional, and sometimes nationalist character of the communities to which they consider themselves ethically bound and whose specific community norms are treated as ethically binding. They valorize nearness as a condition for encountering and knowing the other and so tend to figure ethical relations as binding upon those whose faces we can see, whose names we can know and pronounce, whom we can already recognize, whose forms and faces are familiar. It is often assumed that proximity imposes certain immediate demands for honoring principles of bodily integrity, nonviolence, and territorial or property rights claims. And yet, it seems to me that something different is happening when one part of the globe rises in moral outrage against actions and events that happen in another part of the globe, a form of moral outrage that does not depend upon a shared language or a common life grounded in physical proximity. In such cases, we are seeing and enacting the very activity of bonds of solidarity that emerge across space and time.

These are times when, in spite of ourselves and quite apart from any intentional act, we are nevertheless solicited by images of distant suffering in ways that compel our concern and move us to act, that is, to voice our objection and register our resistance to such violence through concrete political means. In this way, we might say that we do not merely or only receive information from the media on the basis of which we, as individuals, then decide to do or not to do anything. We do not only consume, and we are not only paralyzed by the surfeit of images. Sometimes, not always, the images that are imposed upon us operate as an ethical solicitation. I want for the moment to call attention to this formulation, since I am trying to underscore that something impinges upon us, without our being able to anticipate or prepare for it in advance, and this means that we are in such moments affronted by something that is beyond our will, not of our making, that comes to us from the outside, as an imposition but also as an ethical demand. I want to suggest that these are ethical obligations that do not require our consent, and neither are they the result of contracts or agreements into which any of us have deliberately entered.

To make this view plain, I want to suggest, as a point of departure, that images and accounts of war suffering are a particular form of ethical solicitation, one that compels us to negotiate questions of proximity and distance. They implicitly formulate ethical quandaries: Is what is happening so far away from me that I can bear no responsibility for it? Is what is happening so close to me that I cannot bear having to take responsibility for it? If I myself did not make this suffering, am I still in some other sense responsible to it? How do we approach these questions? Although what I have to offer here will not be focused on photographs or images, I want to suggest that the ethical solicitation that we encounter in, say, the photograph of war suffering brings up larger questions about ethical obligation. After all, we do not always choose to see the images of war, of violence and death, and we can reject them vehemently. After all, who put this image in my face, and what are they trying to make me feel, or what are they trying to do to me? Indeed, we might understand this as the structural paranoia of the image, the way it is bound up with an indefinite form of address. But even the paranoid is being solicited in some way or attests to the fact that he or she is being addressed in some way. Is there a Levinasian undercurrent in this moment of having to listen to the voice of someone we never chose to hear or to see an image that we never elected to see?

Such images may appear on our screen, or we may flash upon them (or they may flash upon us) as we walk down the street by the kiosks where newspapers are sold. We can click on a site as a deliberate act in order to get the news, but that does not mean that we are actually prepared for what we see, and it does not even mean that we have chosen to expose ourselves to what impinges upon us visually or aurally. We understand what it means to be overloaded or overwhelmed with sensory images, but are we also ethically overwhelmed at such instances, and would it be a problem if we were not? Susan Sontag made the point that war photography overwhelms and paralyzes us at the same time, and she actively wondered whether we might still rely on the image to incite a political deliberation on—and resistance to—the unjust character of state violence and war.[1] But is it possible that we might be overwhelmed and unparalyzed—and can we understand that as the working of an ethical obligation upon our sensibilities? Indeed, this word, sensibility, is the one that Levinas reserves for that region of responsiveness that precedes the ego, a kind of response that therefore is and is not my response. To say it is my response is to lodge the ego as its source, but what we are trying to talk about is a form of responsiveness that implies a dispossession of the egological. With this in mind, I return to my question: Must we, in fact, be overwhelmed to some degree in order to have motive for action? We only act when we are moved to act, and we are moved by something that affects us from the outside, from elsewhere, from the lives of others, imposing a surfeit that we act from and upon. According to such a view of ethical obligation, receptivity is not only a precondition for action but one of its constituent features. The term "media" names any mode of presentation that relays to us some version of reality from the outside; it operates by means of a series of foreclosures that make possible what we might call its message, which impinges on us, by which I mean both the foreclosure—what is edited out, what is outside the margins—and what is presented. When we find ourselves in the midst of a responsive action of some kind, we are usually responding to what we have not chosen to see (what is barred from our seeing but also what is given in the domain of visual appearance). It may seem like something of a leap, but I want to suggest that this very brief account of what is unchosen in the force of the image articulates something about ethical obligations that impose themselves upon us without our consent. So if we are open to this point, though we have reason enough not to accept it fully, it would seem to suggest that consent is not a sufficient ground for delimiting the global obligations that form our responsibility. In fact, responsibility may well be implicated in a vast domain of the nonconsensual.

My second point, however, is to contest the notion that ethical obligations emerge only in the contexts of established communities that are gathered within borders, are unified by the same language, and/or constitute a people or a nation. Obligations to those who are far away, as well as to those who are proximate, cross linguistic and national boundaries and are only possible by virtue of visual or linguistic translations, which include temporal and spatial dislocations. These kinds of circuits confound any communitarian basis for delimiting the global obligations that we have. So my proposal is that neither consent nor communitarianism will justify or delimit the range of obligations that I seek to address here. I think this is probably an experience we have in relation to the media when it brings suffering at a distance very close and makes what is proximate appear very far away. My own thesis is that the ethical demands that emerge through the global circuits in these times depend on this limited but necessary reversibility of proximity and distance. Indeed, I want to suggest that certain bonds are actually wrought through this very reversibility and the impasse through which it is constituted. This very reversibility dead-ends, as it were, in the problem of corporeal locatedness, since no matter how fully transported through media we might be, we are also emphatically not. So if we are filmed on the street, the body and the street transport to some degree, acquiring potentially global dimensions; and yet that report and transport are only intelligible on the assumption that some dimensions of the time and space of that bodily location cannot be transported, are left there, or persist there and have an obdurate thereness. But I will return to this problem of the body down the line, since I have no other choice, and perhaps none of us really do.

For now, I want only to suggest in a fairly elementary way that if I am only bound to those who are close to me, already familiar, then my ethics are invariably parochial, communitarian, and exclusionary. If I am only bound to those who are "human" in the abstract, then I avert every effort to translate culturally between my own situation and that of others. If I am only bound to those who suffer at a distance, and never those who are close to me, then I evacuate my situation in an effort to secure the distance that allows me to entertain ethical feeling and even feel myself to be ethical. But ethical relations are mediated—and I use that word deliberately here, invoking a reading of Hegel in the midst of the digital age. And this means that questions of location are confounded such that what is happening "there" also happens in some sense "here," and if what is happening "there" depends on the event being registered in several "elsewheres," then it would seem that the ethical claim of the event takes place always in a "here" and "there" that are in some ways reversible; but that reversibility finds its limit in the fact that the body cannot be relieved of its locatedness, its exposure, through its mediated transport. In one sense, the event is emphatically local, since it is precisely the people there whose bodies are at risk. But if those bodies on the line are not registered elsewhere, there is no global response, and also no global form of ethical recognition and connection, and so something of the reality of the event is lost. It is not just that one discrete population views another through certain media moments but that such a response makes evident a form of global connectedness, however provisional, with those whose lives and actions are registered in this way. In short, to be unprepared for the media image that overwhelms can lead not to paralysis but to a situation of (a) being moved, and so acting precisely by virtue of being acted upon, and (b) being at once there and here, and, in different ways, accepting and negotiating the multilocality and cross temporality of ethical connections we might rightly call global.

Can we, then, turn to some versions of ethical philosophy in order to reformulate what it means to register an ethical demand during these times that is reducible neither to consent nor to agreement and that takes place outside of established community bonds? I will consider briefly some arguments by Emmanuel Levinas and Hannah Arendt on these vexed relations that hold among ethics, proximity, and distance. My choice of two thinkers who are in part formed through Jewish intellectual traditions (Levinas) and Jewish historical situations (Arendt) is not accidental. In a separate project that casts its shadow here, I am trying to articulate a version of cohabitation that follows from the account of ethical obligation I am describing; both of these thinkers offer views that are both illuminating and problematic for this task. I hope to make matters more concrete by turning to Palestine/Israel toward the end of my remarks, mainly to suggest a set of

Jewish views on cohabitation that demands a departure from communitarianism, even Jewish communitarianism, and that may serve as a critical alternative during this time when the state of Israel seeks to secure its claim to represent Jewishness. Luckily for you, and perhaps for me as well, that last concern will not be the center of my remarks here, even though, in all fairness, it does constitute the central argument of my recent work.

Levinas

There are two dissonant dimensions of Levinas's ethical philosophy. On the one hand, there is the importance of the category of proximity to his idea of ethical relations. Indeed, it seems that the ways that others act upon us, without our will, constitute the occasion of an ethical appeal or solicitation. This means that we are acted on, and solicited, ethically, prior to any clear sense of choice. To be impinged upon by another assumes a bodily proximity, and if it is the "face" that acts upon us, then we are to some extent affected and claimed by that "face" at the same time. On the other hand, our ethical obligations extend to those who are not proximate in any physical sense and who do not have to be part of a recognizable community to which we both belong. Indeed, for Levinas, those who act upon us are clearly other to us; it is precisely not by virtue of their sameness that we are bound to them.

Of course, Levinas sustained some contradictory views on this question of the otherness of the other who makes an ethical claim on me: he clearly affirmed forms of nationalism, especially Israeli nationalism, and also held to the notion that only within a Judeo-Christian tradition were ethical relations possible. But let us, for the moment, read him against himself, or read him for the political possibilities he opens up, even those he never intended. Levinas's position allows us the following conclusion: that the set of ethical values by which one population is bound to another in no way depends on those two populations bearing similar marks of national, cultural, religious, or racial belonging. It is interesting that Levinas insisted that we are bound to those we do not know, and even those we did not choose, could never have chosen, and that these obligations are, strictly speaking, precontractual. And yet, he was the one who claimed in an interview that the Palestinian had no face and that he only meant to extend ethical obligations to those who were bound together by his version of Judeo-Christian and classical Greek origins.[2] In some ways, he gave us the very principle that he betrayed. His failure directly contradicts his formulation of the demand to be ethically responsive to those who exceed our immediate sphere of belonging but to whom we nevertheless belong, regardless of any question of what we choose or by what contracts we are bound or what established forms of cultural belonging are available.

Of course, this raises the question of how there can be an ethical relation to those who cannot appear within the horizon of ethics, who are not persons or are not considered to be the kinds of beings with whom one can or must enter into an ethical relation. Is it possible to take the ethical philosophy formulated there and deploy it against the very exclusionary assumptions by which it is sometimes supported? Can we, in other words, use Levinas against himself to help in the articulation of a global ethics that would extend beyond the religious and cultural communities that he saw as its necessary condition and limit?

Let us take as an example his argument that ethical relations are asymmetrical. In his work, the other has priority over me. What

does that concretely mean? Does the other not have the same obligation toward me? Why should I be obligated toward another
who does not reciprocate in the same way toward me? For Levinas,
reciprocity cannot be the basis of ethics, since ethics is not a bar-
gain: it cannot be the case that my ethical relation to another is
contingent on his or her ethical relation to me, since that would
make that ethical relation less than absolute and binding, and it
would establish my self-preservation as a distinct and bounded sort
of being as more primary than any relation I have to another. For
Levinas, no ethics can be derived from egoism; indeed, egoism is
the defeat of ethics itself.

I take distance from Levinas here, since, though I agree in the
refutation of the primacy of self-preservation for ethical thinking,
I want to insist upon a certain intertwinement between that other
life, all those other lives, and my own—one that is irreducible to
national belonging or communitarian affiliation. In my view
(which is surely not mine alone), the life of the other, the life that
is not our own, is also our life, since whatever sense "our" life has
is derived precisely from this sociality, this being already, and from
the start, dependent on a world of others, constituted in and by a
social world. In this way, there are surely others distinct from me
whose ethical claim upon me is irreducible to an egoistic calculation on my part. But that is because we are, however distinct, also
bound to one another and to living processes that exceed human
form. And this is not always a happy or felicitous experience. To
find that one's life is also the life of others, even as this life is distinct and must be distinct, means that one's boundary is at once a
limit and a site of adjacency, a mode of spatial and temporal nearness and even boundedness. Moreover, the bounded and living
appearance of the body is the condition of being exposed to the

other; exposed to solicitation, seduction, passion, and injury; exposed in ways that sustain us but also in ways that can destroy us. In this sense the exposure of the body points to its precariousness. At the same time, for Levinas, this precarious and corporeal being is responsible for the life of the other, which means that no matter how much one fears for one's own life, preserving the life of the other is paramount. If only the Israeli army felt this way! Indeed, this is a form of responsibility that is not easy to assume while undergoing a felt sense of precarity. Precarity names both the necessity and the difficulty of ethics.

What is the relation between precarity and vulnerability? It is surely hard to feel at once vulnerable to destruction by the other and also responsible for the other, and readers of Levinas object all the time to his formulation that we are, all of us, in some sense responsible for that which persecutes us. He does not mean that we bring about our persecution—not at all. Rather, "persecution" is the strange and disconcerting name that Levinas gives to an ethical demand that imposes itself upon us against our will. We are, despite ourselves, open to this imposition, and though it overrides our will, its shows us that the claims that others make upon us are part of our very sensibility, our receptivity, and our answerability. We are, in other words, called upon, and this is only possible because we are in some sense vulnerable to claims that we cannot anticipate in advance and for which there is no adequate preparation. For Levinas, there is no other way to understand the ethical reality; ethical obligation not only depends upon our vulnerability to the claims of others but also establishes us as creatures who are fundamentally defined by that ethical relation. This ethical relation is not a virtue that I have or exercise; it is prior to any individual sense of self. It is not as discrete individuals that we honor this ethical relation. I am already bound to you, and this is what it means to be the self I am, receptive to you in ways that I cannot fully predict or control. This is also, clearly, the condition of my injurability as well, and in this way my answerability and my injurability are bound up with one another. In other words, you may frighten me and threaten me, but my obligation to you must remain firm.

This relation precedes individuation, and when I act ethically, I am undone as a bounded being. I come apart. I find that I am my relation to the "you" whose life I seek to preserve, and without that relation, this "I" makes no sense and has lost its mooring in this ethics that is always prior to the ontology of the ego. Another way to put this point is that the "I" becomes undone in its ethical relation to the "you," which means that there is a very specific mode of being dispossessed that makes ethical relationality possible. If I possess myself too firmly or too rigidly, I cannot be in an ethical relation. The ethical relation means ceding a certain egological perspective for one that is structured fundamentally by a mode of address: you call upon me, and I answer. But if I answer, it is only because I was already answerable; that is, this susceptibility and vulnerability constitutes me at the most fundamental level and is there, we might say, prior to any deliberate decision to answer the call. In other words, one has to be already capable of receiving the call before actually answering it. In this sense, ethical responsibility presupposes ethical responsiveness.

Arendt

Most scholars would want to keep any consideration of Emmanuel Levinas separate from an analysis of Hannah Arendt: He is a phi-

losopher of ethics, drawing on religious traditions, and he emphasizes the ethical importance of passivity and receptivity; she is a social and political philosopher, adamantly secular, who emphasizes
time and again the political value of action. Why bring a discussion of Levinas together with one regarding Arendt? Both Levinas
and Arendt take issue with the classically liberal conception of
individualism, that is, the idea that individuals knowingly enter
into certain contracts, and their obligation follows from having
deliberately and volitionally entered into agreements with one
another. This view assumes that we are only responsible for those
relations, codified by agreements, into which we have knowingly
and volitionally entered. And Arendt disputes this view. Indeed,
it was the substance of the argument that she made against Adolf
Eichmann. He thought he could choose which populations should
live and die, and in this sense he thought he could choose with
whom to cohabit the earth. What he failed to understand, according to Arendt, is that no one has the prerogative to choose
with whom to cohabit the earth. We can choose in some ways how
and where to live, and in local ways we can choose with whom
to live. But if we were to decide with whom to cohabit the earth,
we would be deciding which portion of humanity may live and
which may die. If that choice is barred to us, that means that we
are under an obligation to live with those who already exist, and
that any choice about who may or may not live is always a genocidal practice; and though we cannot dispute that genocide has
happened, and happens still, we are wrong to think that freedom
in any ethical sense is ever compatible with the freedom to commit
genocide. The unchosen character of earthly cohabitation is, for
Arendt, the condition of our very existence as ethical and political
beings. Hence, to exercise that prerogative of genocide is not only

to destroy political conditions of personhood but to destroy freedom itself, understood not as an individual act but as a plural action. Without that plurality against which we cannot choose, we have no freedom and, therefore, no choice. This means that there is an unchosen condition of freedom and that, in being free, we affirm something about what is unchosen for us. If freedom seeks to exceed that unfreedom that is its condition, then we destroy plurality and we jeopardize, in her view, our status as persons, considered as *zoon politikon*. This was one argument that Arendt made about why the death penalty was justified for Eichmann. In her view, Eichmann had already destroyed himself by not realizing that his own life was bound to those he destroyed, and individual life makes no sense, has no reality, outside of the social and political framework in which all lives are equally valued.[3]

In *Eichmann in Jerusalem* (1963), Arendt argues that Eichmann and his superiors failed to realize that the heterogeneity of the earth's population is an irreversible condition of social and political life itself.[4] So Arendt's accusation against Eichmann bespeaks a firm conviction that none of us may exercise such a prerogative, that those with whom we cohabit the earth are given to us, prior to choice and so prior to any social or political contracts we might enter into through deliberation and volition. In Eichmann's case, the effort to choose with whom to cohabit the earth was an explicit effort to annihilate some part of the population—Jews, gypsies, homosexuals, communists, the disabled, and the ill, among others—and so the exercise of freedom upon which he insisted was genocide. Not only is this choice an attack on cohabitation as a precondition of political life in Arendt's view, but it commits us to the following proposition: we must devise institutions and policies that actively preserve and affirm the unchosen character of open-ended and plural cohabitation. Not only do we live with those we never chose and with whom we may feel no immediate sense of social belonging, but we are also obligated to preserve those lives and the open-ended plurality that is the global population.

Although Arendt would doubtless dispute my view, I think what she has offered is an ethical view of cohabitation that serves as a guideline for particular forms of politics. In this sense, concrete political norms and policies emerge from the unchosen character of these modes of cohabitation. The necessity of cohabiting the earth is a principle that, in her philosophy, must guide the actions and policies of any neighborhood, community, or nation. The decision to live in one community or another is surely justified as long as it does not imply that those who live outside the community do not deserve to live. In other words, every communitarian ground for belonging is only justifiable on the condition that it is subordinate to a noncommunitarian opposition to genocide. The way I read this, every inhabitant who belongs to a community belongs also to the earth—a notion she clearly takes from Heidegger—and this implies a commitment not only to every other inhabitant of that earth but, we can surely add, to sustaining the earth itself. And with this last proviso, I seek to offer an ecological supplement to Arendt's anthropocentrism.

In *Eichmann in Jerusalem,* Arendt speaks not only for the Jews but for any and every other minority who would be expelled from habitation on the earth by another group. The one implies the other, and the "speaking for" universalizes the founding interdiction even as it does not override the plurality whose life it seeks to protect. One reason Arendt refuses to separate the Jews from the other so-called nations persecuted by the Nazis is that she is arguing in the name of a plurality coextensive with human life in any and all of its cultural forms. At the same time, her judgment of Eichmann is one that emerges precisely from the historical situation of a diasporic Jew who was herself a refugee from Nazi Germany, but who also objected to the Israeli courts representing a specific nation, when the crime, in her view, was a crime against humanity, and to the courts representing only the Jewish victims of the genocide, when there were many other groups annihilated and displaced in accord with the Nazi policy formulated and implemented by Eichmann and his cohorts.

This same notion of unchosen cohabitation implies not only the irreversibly plural or heterogeneous character of the earth's population, and an obligation to safeguard that plurality, but also a commitment to an equal right to inhabit the earth and so a commitment to equality as well. These two dimensions of her discussion took specific historical form in her argument against the idea of Israel as a state based on principles of Jewish sovereignty and for a federated Palestine in the late 1940s. The political conception of plurality for which she fought was, in her view, implicit in the American Revolution, and it led her to refuse to accept exclusively national, racial, or religious grounds for citizenship. Moreover, she objected to the founding of any state that required the expulsion of its inhabitants and the production of a new refugee class, especially when such a state invoked the rights of refugees to legitimate its founding.

Arendt's normative views are these: there is no one part of the population that can claim the earth for itself, no community or nation-state or regional unit, no clan, no party, and no race. This means that unwilled proximity and unchosen cohabitation are preconditions of our political existence, the basis of her critique of nationalism, the obligation to live on the earth and in a polity that establishes equality for a population necessarily and irreversibly heterogeneous. Indeed, unwilled proximity and unchosen cohabitation also serve as the basis of our obligations not to destroy any part of the human population and to outlaw genocide as a crime against humanity, but also to invest institutions with the demand to seek to make all lives livable and equally so. Thus, from unchosen cohabitation, Arendt derives notions of universality and equality that commit us to institutions that seek to sustain human lives without regarding some part of the population as socially dead, as redundant, or as intrinsically unworthy of life and therefore ungrievable.

Arendt's views on cohabitation, federated authority, equality, and universality, elaborated from the 1940s through the 1960s, stood in stark contrast to those who were defending nationalist forms of Jewish sovereignty, differential classifications for Jewish and non-Jewish citizens, military policies to uproot Palestinians from their lands, and efforts to establish a Jewish demographic majority for the state. It is often taught that Israel became a historical and ethical necessity for the Jews during and after the Nazi genocide, and that anyone who questions the founding principles of the Jewish state shows an extraordinary insensitivity to the plight of the Jews; but there were Jewish thinkers and political activists at the time, including Arendt, Martin Buber, Hans Kohn, and Judah Magnes, who thought that among the most important lessons of the Nazi genocide was an opposition to illegitimate state violence, to any state formation that sought to give electoral priority and citizenship to one race or religion, and that nation-states ought to be internationally barred from dispossessing whole populations who fail to fit the purified idea of the nation.

For those who extrapolated principles of justice from the historical experience of internment and dispossession, the political aim is to extend equality regardless of cultural background or formation, across languages and religions, to those none of us ever chose (or did not recognize that we chose) and with whom we have an enduring obligation to find a way to live. For whoever "we" are, we are also those who were never chosen, who emerge on this earth without everyone's consent, and who belong, from the start, to a wider population and a sustainable earth. And this condition, paradoxically, yields the radical potential for new modes of sociality and politics beyond the avid and wretched bonds formed through settler colonialism and expulsion. We are all, in this sense, the unchosen, but we are nevertheless unchosen together. It is not uninteresting to note that Arendt, herself a Jew and refugee, understood her obligation not to belong to the "chosen people" but, rather, to the unchosen, and to make mixed community precisely among those whose existence implies a right to exist and to lead a livable life.

Alternative Jewishness, Precarious Life

I have offered you two perspectives derived in different ways from Jewishness. Levinas was a self-avowed Jewish thinker and a Zionist, deriving his account of responsibility from an understanding of the commandments, how they act upon us and how they compel us ethically. And Arendt, though surely not religious, nevertheless took her position as a Jewish refugee from World War II as a point of departure for thinking about genocide, statelessness, and the plural conditions of political life.

Of course, neither Levinas nor Arendt is easy to work with to establish a set of political ideals for Israel/Palestine. As with Levinas, there are parts of Arendt's position that are clearly racist (she objected, for instance, to Arab Jews, identified as a European, and saw Jewishness restrictively within those terms), and yet some of what she writes is still a resource for thinking about the current global obligations to oppose and resist genocide, the reproduction of stateless populations, and the importance of struggling for an open-ended conception of plurality.[5]

ARENDT'S EURO-AMERICAN FRAMEWORK was clearly limited, and yet another limitation becomes clear if we try to understand the relationship of precarity to practices of cohabitation. For Arendt, the needs of the body are to be relegated to the private sphere. Precarity only makes sense if we are able to identify bodily dependency and need, hunger and the need for shelter, the vulnerability to injury and destruction, forms of social trust that let us live and thrive, and the passions linked to our very persistence as clearly political issues. If Arendt thought that such matters had to be relegated to the private realm, Levinas understood the importance of vulnerability but failed to really link vulnerability to a politics of the body. Although Levinas seems to presuppose a body impinged upon, he does not give it an explicit place in his ethical philosophy. And though Arendt theorizes the problem of the body, of the located body, the speaking body emerging into the "space of appearance" as part of any account of political action, she is not quite willing to affirm a politics that struggles to overcome inequalities in food distribution, that affirms rights of housing, and that targets inequalities in the sphere of reproductive labor.

In my view, some ethical claims emerge from bodily life, and perhaps all ethical claims presuppose a bodily life, understood as injurable, one that is not restrictively human. After all, the life that is worth preserving and safeguarding, that should be protected from murder (Levinas) and genocide (Arendt), is connected to, and dependent upon, nonhuman life in essential ways; this follows from the idea of the human animal, as Derrida has articulated it, which becomes a different point of departure for thinking about politics. If we try to understand in concrete terms what it means to commit ourselves to preserving the life of the other, we are invariably confronted with the bodily conditions of life and so to a commitment not only to the other's corporeal persistence but to all those environmental conditions that make life livable.

In the so-called private sphere delineated in Arendt's *The Human Condition,* we find the question of needs, the reproduction of the material conditions of life, and the problems of transience, reproduction, and death alike—everything that pertains to precarious life. The possibility of whole populations being annihilated through either genocidal policies or systemic negligence follows not only from the fact that there are those who believe that they can decide with whom they will inhabit the earth, but also because such thinking presupposes a disavowal of an irreducible fact of politics: the vulnerability to destruction by others that follows from a condition of precarity in all modes of political and social interdependency. We can make this into a broad existential claim, namely, that everyone is precarious, and this follows from our social existence as bodily beings who depend upon one another for shelter and sustenance and who, therefore, are at risk of statelessness, homelessness, and destitution under unjust and unequal political conditions. As much as I am making such a claim, I am also making another, namely, that our precarity is to a large extent dependent upon the organization of economic and social relationships, the presence or absence of sustaining infrastructures and social and political institutions. So as soon as the existential claim is articulated in its specificity, it ceases to be existential. And since it must be articulated in its specificity, it was never existential. In this sense, precarity is indissociable from that dimension of politics that addresses the organization and protection of bodily needs. Precarity exposes our sociality, the fragile and necessary dimensions of our interdependency.

Whether explicitly stated or not, every political effort to manage populations involves a tactical distribution of precarity, more often than not articulated through an unequal distribution of precarity, one that depends on dominant norms regarding whose life is grievable and worth protecting and whose life is ungrievable, or marginally or episodically grievable, and so, in that sense, already lost in part or in whole, and thus less worthy of protection and sustenance. My point is not to rehabilitate humanism but, rather, to struggle for a conception of ethical obligation that is grounded in precarity. No one escapes the precarious dimension of social life—it is, we might say, the joint of our nonfoundation. And we cannot understand cohabitation without understanding that a generalized precarity obligates us to oppose genocide and to sustain life on egalitarian terms. Perhaps this feature of our lives can serve as the basis for the right of protection against genocide, whether through deliberate or negligent means. After all, even though our interdependency constitutes us as more than thinking beings, indeed as social and embodied, vulnerable and passionate, our thinking gets nowhere without the presupposition of the interdependent and sustaining conditions of life.

We might think that interdependency is a happy or promising notion, but it is often the condition for territorial wars and forms of state violence. Indeed, I am not sure that we have yet been able to think about the unmanageability of dependency at the level of politics—to what fear, panic, repulsion, violence, and domination it can lead. It is true that I am trying to struggle toward an affirmation of interdependency in what I have offered here, but I am trying to underscore just how difficult it is to struggle for social and political forms that are committed to fostering a sustainable interdependency on egalitarian terms. When any of us are affected by the sufferings of others, it is not only that we put ourselves in their place or that they usurp our own place; perhaps it is the moment in which a certain chiasmic link comes to the fore and I become somehow implicated in lives that are clearly not the same as my own. And this happens even when we do not know the names of those who make their appeal to us or when we struggle to pronounce the name or to speak in a language we have never learned. At their best, some media representations of suffering at a distance compel us to give up our more narrow communitarian ties and to respond, sometimes in spite of ourselves, sometimes even against our will, to a perceived injustice. Such presentations can bring the fate of others near or make it seem very far away, and yet, the kinds of ethical demands that emerge through the media in these times depend on this reversibility of proximity and distance. Indeed, certain bonds are actually wrought through this very reversibility, however incomplete it is. And we might find ways of understanding the interdependency that characterizes cohabitation precisely as these bonds. For if I am here and there, I am also not ever fully there, and even if I am here, I am always more than fully here. Is there a way to understand this reversibility as limited by bodily time and space in such a way that the other is not radically other, and I am not radically over here as an I, but the link, the joint, is chiasmic and only and always partly reversible and partly not?

There are, as we know, antagonistic ties, wretched bonds, raging and mournful modes of connectedness. In those cases, living with others on adjacent lands or on contested or colonized lands produces aggression and hostility in the midst of that cohabitation. The mode of unchosen cohabitation that belongs to the colonized is surely not the same as the notion of a democratic plurality established on grounds of equality. But they both have their mode of wretched attachment and adjacency.[6]

Even in situations of antagonistic and unchosen modes of cohabitation, certain ethical obligations emerge. First, since we do not choose with whom to cohabit the earth, we have to honor those obligations to preserve the lives of those we may not love, those we may never love, do not know, and did not choose. Second, these obligations emerge from the social conditions of political life, not from any agreement we have made or from any deliberate choice. And yet, these very social conditions of livable life are precisely those that have to be achieved. We cannot rely on them as presuppositions that will guarantee our good life together. On the contrary, they supply the ideals toward which we must struggle, which involves a passage through the problem of violence. Because we are bound to realize these conditions; we are also bound to one another, in passionate and fearful alliance, often in spite of ourselves, but ultimately for ourselves, for a "we" who is constantly in the making. Third, these conditions imply equality, as Arendt tells us, but also an exposure to precarity (a point derived from Levinas), which leads us to understand a global obligation imposed upon us to find political and economic forms that minimize precarity and establish economic political equality. Those forms of cohabitation characterized by equality and minimized precarity become the goal to be achieved by any struggle against subjugation and exploitation, but also the goal that starts to be achieved in the practices of alliances that assemble across distances to achieve that very goal. We struggle in, from, and against precarity. Thus, it is not from pervasive love for humanity or a pure desire for peace that we strive to live together. We live together because we have no choice, and though we sometimes rail against that unchosen condition, we remain obligated to struggle to affirm the ultimate value of that unchosen social world, an affirmation that is not quite a choice, a struggle that makes itself known and felt precisely when we exercise freedom in a way that is necessarily committed to the equal value of lives. We can be alive or dead to the sufferings of others—they can be dead or alive to us. But it is only when we understand that what happens there also happens here, and that "here" is already an elsewhere, and necessarily so, that we stand a chance of grasping the difficult and shifting global connections in ways that let us know the transport and the constraint of what we might still call ethics.

Chapter 4

Bodily Vulnerability, Coalitional Politics

I propose to begin this chapter by focusing on three issues: bodily vulnerability, coalitions, and street politics—but perhaps not quite to string them together in a fully obvious way. And then I would like to turn to a consideration of vulnerability as a form of activism, or as that which is in some sense mobilized in forms of resistance. As we all know, politics does not always happen on the street; politics does not always foreground vulnerability, and coalitions can be made from any number of dispositions, not necessarily a shared sense of vulnerability. Indeed, our skepticism about vulnerability is, I wager, quite enormous. Women have too long been associated with vulnerability, and there is no clear way to derive an ethics, much less a politics, from that notion. So I concede at the outset that I have a great deal of work to do by suggesting that these three ideas might usefully inform one another and lead usefully to a consideration of vulnerability.

My increasingly urgent sense about speaking in public, or writing for a public, is not that it should lead us straightway to a path for action; it is, rather, a chance to pause together and reflect on the conditions and directions of acting, a form of reflecting that has its own value, and not merely an instrumental one. Indeed, whether or not this kind of pausing is itself part of action and activism is another question, but my considered impulse is to say, yes, it is, but not only, or not exclusively. On this occasion, I want to think about these topics in order to set aside some of the misconceptions that could easily arise. For instance, given racist mobs and violent attacks, I am certainly not saying that all bodies collected in the street are a good thing or that we should celebrate mass demonstrations, or that bodies assembled form a certain ideal of community or even a new politics worthy of praise. Though sometimes bodies assembled on the street are clearly cause for joy and even hope—and surging crowds sometimes do become the occasion for revolutionary hopefulness—let us remember that the phrase "bodies on the street" can refer equally well to right-wing demonstrations, to military soldiers assembled to quell demonstrations or seize power, to lynch mobs or anti-immigrant populist movements taking over public space. So they are neither intrinsically good nor intrinsically bad; they assume differing values depending on what they are assembled for, and how that assembly works. And yet, the idea of bodies on the street together gives leftists a bit of a thrill, as if power were being taken back, taken away, assumed and incorporated in some way that portends democracy. I understand that thrill, have even written from it, but here I will review some of my doubts, some of which I suspect are shared.

From the outset, we have to be prepared to ask: Under what conditions do we find bodies assembled on the street to be cause for celebration, or, what forms of assembly actually work in the service of realizing greater ideals of justice and equality, even the realization of democracy itself?[1]

Minimally, we can say that those demonstrations that seek to realize justice and equality are worthy of praise. But of course, we are called upon to define our terms, since, as we know, there are conflicting views of justice, and there are surely many disparate ways of thinking about and valuing equality. Another problem immediately presents itself: in certain parts of the world, political alliances do not, or cannot, take the form of street assemblies, and there are important reasons for this. We need only consider conditions of intense police surveillance or military occupation that keep people off streets or out of markets. In those instances, crowds cannot swell on the streets without risking imprisonment, injury, or death, and so alliances are sometimes made in other forms, ones that seek to find ways to minimize bodily exposure as demands for justice are made. Hunger strikes within prisons, such as those that took place in Palestine in the spring of 2012 and continue sporadically, also constitute forms of resistance that are forcibly restricted to confined spaces, where bodies in parallel forms of isolation make demands for freedom, for due process, for the rights to move in public space and to exercise public freedoms. So let us remember that bodily exposure can take different forms: heightened bodily exposure happens when assemblies deliberately expose their bodies to police power on the street or in public domains. It is also what happens daily under conditions of occupation, when walking down the street or trying to pass through a checkpoint, making the body available to harassment, injury, detention, or death; and yet other forms of bodily exposure take place within prisons, detention camps, and refugee camps, where military and police personnel exercise both the power of surveillance and the power to arrest action, to make use of force, to enforce isolation, and to determine how and when one eats or sleeps, and under what conditions. So obviously the point is not to claim that bodily exposure is always a political good or even the most successful strategy for an emancipatory movement. Sometimes overcoming unwilled conditions of bodily exposure is precisely the aim of a political struggle. And sometimes deliberately exposing the body to possible harm is part of the very meaning of political resistance.

Of course, we have to consider as well that some forms of political assembly do not take place on the street or in the square, precisely because streets and squares do not exist or do not form the symbolic center of that political action. For instance, a movement may be galvanized for the purposes of establishing adequate infrastructure—we can think about the continuing shantytowns or townships of South Africa, Kenya, and Pakistan; the temporary shelters constructed along the borders of Europe; and also the barrios of Venezuela or the barracas of Portugal. Such spaces are populated by groups of people, including immigrants, squatters, and Roma, who are struggling just for running and clean water, working toilets, sometimes a closed door on public toilets, paved streets, paid work, and necessary provisions. So the street is not always a site that we can take for granted as the public ground for certain kinds of public assemblies; the street, as public space and thoroughfare, is also a public good for which people fight—an infrastructural necessity that forms one of the demands of certain forms of popular mobilization. The street is not just the basis or platform for a political demand, but an infrastructural good. And so when assemblies gather in public spaces in order to fight against the decimation of infrastructural goods, to fight against austerity measures, for instance, that would undercut public education, libraries, transit systems, and roads, we find that sometimes the fight is for the platform itself. In other words, we cannot even fight for infrastructural goods without being able to assume them to one degree or another, so when infrastructural conditions for politics are themselves decimated, so too are the assemblies that depend upon them. At such a point, the condition of the political is one of the goods for which political assembly takes place—this might be the double meaning of the infrastructural under conditions in which public goods are increasingly dismantled by privatization.[2]

In effect, the demand for infrastructure is a demand for a certain kind of inhabitable ground, and its meaning and force derive precisely from that lack. This is why the demand is not for all kinds of infrastructure, since some serve the decimation of livable life (military forms of detention, imprisonment, occupation, and surveillance, for instance), and some support livable life. In some cases, the street cannot be taken for granted as the space of appearance, the Arendtian space of politics, since there is, as we know, a struggle to establish that very ground, or to take that ground back from police control.[3] The possibility of doing that, however, depends upon the performative efficacy of creating a political space from existing infrastructural conditions. Arendt is at least partially right when she claims that the space of appearance comes into being at the moment of political action. A romantic thought to be sure, since it is not always so easy to do in practice. She presumes that the material conditions for gathering are separate from any particular space of appearance, but the task is actually to let the infrastructure become part of the new action, even a collaborative actor. But if politics is oriented toward the making and preserving of the conditions that allow for livability, then it seems that the space of appearance is not ever fully separable from questions of infrastructure and architecture, and that they not only condition the action, but take part in the making of the space of politics.

Of course, the street is not the only infrastructural support for political speech and action. It is also a major issue and object for political mobilization. In a sense, we already know the idea that freedom can only be exercised if there is a support for freedom, understood sometimes as a material condition that makes that exercise possible and powerful. Indeed, the body that exercises speech or moves through space, across borders, is presumed to be one that can speak and move. A body that is both supported and agentic is presumed as a necessary condition for other sorts of mobilizations. Indeed, the very term "mobilization" depends on an operative sense of mobility, itself a right, one that many people cannot take for granted. For the body to move, it must usually have a surface of some kind (unless it is swimming or flying), and it must have at its disposal whatever technical supports allow for movement to take place. So the pavement and the street are already to be understood as requirements of the body as it exercises its rights of mobility. They themselves become part of the action and not only its support.

We could certainly make a list of how this idea of a body, supported and agentic, implicated in the infrastructure that makes movement possible, is at work implicitly or explicitly in any number of political movements: struggles for food and shelter, protection from injury and destruction, the right to work, affordable health care. So, on one level, we are asking about the implicit idea of the body at work in certain kinds of political demands and mobilizations; on another level, we are trying to find out how mobilizations take as their objects of political concern those requirements and supports that are indissociable from what we call the human body. My suggestion is that under conditions in which infrastructures are being decimated, the very platform for politics becomes the object around which political mobilization rallies. And this means that demands made in the name of the body (its protection, shelter, nourishment, mobility, expression) sometimes must take place with and through the body and its technical and infrastructural dimensions. When this happens, it may seem that the body is the means and ends of politics.[4] But the point is precisely to underscore that the body is not isolated from all those conditions, technologies, and life processes that make it possible.

When I speak in this way, it appears that I have sought recourse to an idea of the human body and perhaps its essential needs. But that is not exactly the case. Such an invariant body and its permanent needs would then become the measure by which we judge certain forms of economic and political organization to be sufficient for human flourishing, or insufficient, that is, undermining that flourishing. But if the idea of the body as a ground or measure is usually understood as a singular body (the "we" is that group of people who for the moment agree to consider such a view), even an ideal or typical body, then this runs contrary to the way that the body has to be understood, in my view, in terms of its supporting networks of relations. If we make the matter individual, we can say that every single body has a certain right to food and shelter. Although we universalize in such a statement ("every" body has this right), we also particularize, understanding the body as discrete, as an individual matter, and that individual body is itself a norm of what the body is and how it ought to be conceptualized. Of course that seems quite obviously right, but consider that the idea of this individual bodily subject of rights might fail to capture the sense of vulnerability, exposure, even dependency, that is implied by the right itself, and that corresponds, I would suggest, with an alternative view of the body. In other words, if we accept

that part of what a body is (and this is for the moment an ontological claim) is its dependency on other bodies and networks of
support, then we are suggesting that it is not altogether right to
conceive of individual bodies as completely distinct from one
another. Of course, neither are they blended into some amor-
phous social body, but if we cannot readily conceptualize the
political meaning of the human body without understanding
those relations in which it lives and thrives, we fail to make the best
possible case for the various political ends we seek to achieve.
What I am suggesting is that it is not just that this or that body is
bound up in a network of relations, but that the body, despite its
clear boundaries, or perhaps precisely by virtue of those very
boundaries, is defined by the relations that make its own life and
action possible. As I hope to show, we cannot understand bodily
vulnerability outside of this conception of its constitutive relations to other humans, living processes, and inorganic conditions
and vehicles for living.

Before elaborating on this sense of relationality, I want to advance the idea that vulnerability is also not just a trait or an episodic
disposition of a discrete body, but is, rather, a mode of relationality that time and again calls some aspect of that discreteness into
question. This will matter as we try to talk about political collec-
tions or coalitions, and even when we try to talk about resistance.
Bodies do not come into the world as self-motoring agents; motor
control is established through time; the body is entered into social
life first and foremost under conditions of dependency, as a dependent being, which means that even the first moments or vocalization and movement are responding to a changing set of conditions
for survival. Those conditions include people somewhere, but
not necessarily one other embodied person who, by the way, only

has the means and capacity to feed and shelter if that person is supported as well. This is why caretakers do not only provide support for others, but require their own conditions of support (which means livable conditions of work and rest, of compensation, housing, and health care). The conditions of support for the most vulnerable moments of life are themselves vulnerable, and these conditions are in part infrastructural, in part human, and in part technical. Even if we concede that this may well be true for infants, but maintain some skepticism about the human adult, I want to suggest that no one, however old, ever grows out of this particular condition, characterized as dependent and susceptible. This seems to me to be borne out by the claim that primary ways of organizing care are linked to broader social and political forms of labor and entitlement. That said, are we speaking only about human bodies, and simply continuing a line of thinking that has conventionally linked psychoanalysis to Marxism? I want to say yes and not quite, and for reasons that perhaps Donna Haraway has already explained at length. If we cannot really speak about bodies at all without the environments, the machines, and the complex systems of social interdependency upon which they rely, then all of these nonhuman dimensions of bodily life prove to be constitutive dimensions of human survival and flourishing. Despite the centuries of claims about *Homo erectus,* the human does not stand alone.[5] Obviously there are examples of people of any age who are dependent on machines, and most of us find ourselves dependent on machines or technology at one point or another. Something similar might be said about the noncontingent relation between humans and animals. Human bodies are not distinguished in any absolute way from animal bodies, even though we can easily concede some differences. It will, however, not do to say that the bodily dimension of the human should be regarded as the animal dimension, as a lamentably long tradition in philosophy has been prone to do. The human creature is, after all, already in relation to the animal, and not in the sense that the animal is the "Other" to the human, but because the human is already an animal, even though not exactly like all other animals (indeed, no kind of animal is exactly like all other kinds, and the category of the animal, by definition, allows for that internal variation). Moreover, a large set of life processes cross the human and the animal and maintain a rather steadfast indifference to the distinction between the two. One of Haraway's points is that the forms of dependency between human and animal suggest that in part they are constituted by and through one another. If we take that dependency to be central, then the difference between animal and human becomes secondary (they are both dependent, and they are dependent on each other, depending on each other to be the kinds of beings they are). In this sense, the ontological distinctions among them emerge from the relations that hold among them. So the analytic distinctions we tend to make between machine, human, and animal all rely on a certain covering over of blended or dependent relations.[6]

I began with the claim that we might rethink the relation between bodies, coalitions, and street politics, and I've suggested that some of the nonhuman and infrastructural conditions for human action end up being the very aims of political mobilization, and that this seems to be especially true under conditions in which infrastructural goods are being decimated broadly and quickly. I've suggested as well that bodies are implicated in these kinds of struggles in at least two ways: as both the ground and the aim of politics. Further, I've suggested that we rethink the relationship between the human body and infrastructure so that we might call into question the discreteness and self-sufficiency of the human body imagined in a singular form, but I've also suggested a way of thinking about the human body as a certain kind of dependency on infrastructure, understood complexly as environment, social relations, and networks of support and sustenance that cross the human, animal, and technical divides. After all, even if we come to understand and enumerate the requirements of the body in the name of which people enter into political struggle, are we claiming that political struggle achieves its aims when those requirements are met? Or do we struggle as well for bodies to thrive, for lives to become livable? I'm using one word after the other, searching for a set of related terms as a way of approaching a problem that resists a technical nomenclature; no single word can adequately describe the character and the aim of this human striving, this striving in concert or this striving together that seems to form one meaning of political movement or mobilization.

It seems important to keep all this in play precisely because there are two argumentative trends that are sometimes hard to think in relation to one another. One argument is that bodies should have what they need to survive, for survival is surely a precondition for realizing the broader political aims of life, ones that are distinctly different from survival itself (this was sometimes the view of Hannah Arendt). The other is that there is no political aim that is separable from the just and equitable reproduction of the conditions of life itself, which includes the exercise of freedom. Can we say that we survive precisely in order to live, and so separate survival and life in that way? Or is it rather the case that survival must always be more than survival in order to be livable?[7] After all, some people do survive certain kinds of traumas, but that does not mean that they are living in a full sense. And though I don't know how to distinguish between living in a full and not so full sense, I take it that there is some importance attached to such a distinction. Can we conclude that the demand for survival is bound up with the demand for a livable life? If we are asked what constitutes the conditions of livable life, we have to be able to answer without positing a single or uniform ideal for that life. It is not a matter, in my view, of finding out what "the human" really is or even what a "human life" should be. In fact, it seems to me that the creaturely dimension of human existence holds us back at this moment. After all, to say that humans are animals, too, is not to embrace bestialization as a demeaned or degraded condition, but to rethink the organic and inorganic interrelationships within which anyone recognizably human emerges; in other words, the human animal lets us rethink the very conditions of livability. We do not need any more ideal forms of the human that always imply lesser forms of the same, or that erase from view modes of life that cannot be translated into that norm, making them surely less livable rather than more. But precisely because "the human" continues to be so politically charged, and for those very reasons, it seems we have to rethink its smaller place within a set of relations, so that we can ask after the conditions in which the "human" is differentially recognized.[8] When I say "we" have to think through the category, I am perhaps engaging a humanist conceit of discourse to show that the category still has us in its grip even as we try to shake ourselves loose from its hold.

At the outset, I confessed that I experience a certain thrill, dating back to my adolescent years, when bodies get together in the street, and yet I am quite suspicious of those political views that hold, for instance, that democracy has to be understood as the event of the surging multitude. I don't think so. It seems to me that we have to ask what it is that holds such a group together, what demand is being shared, or what felt sense of injustice and unlivability, what intimation of the possibility of change heightens the collective sense of things. For all that to be democratic, there has to be an opposition to existing and expanding inequalities, to ever-increasing conditions of precarity for many populations both locally and globally, and to forms of authoritarian and securitarian control that seek to suppress democratic processes and movements. Although we sometimes do imagine that political deliberation and action take place in the form of an assembly, there are other ways of conferring and acting that do not presuppose the occupation of the same ground. There are bodies that assemble on the street or online or through other less visible networks of solidarity, especially for prisoners whose political claims are made through forms of solidarity that may or may not appear directly in any one public space, and whose solidarity, when it emerges, rests on a common and forcible exclusion from public space, and a forcible isolation in cells monitored by police or security personnel. This raises the question of what form the freedom of assembly takes when it is explicitly denied as a right. If we say there is no freedom of assembly in prison, or that it is limited, then we certainly acknowledge that those in prison have been forcibly deprived of that freedom, and we can then debate the justice or injustice of having been deprived of that quite essential dimension of citizenship. I am all for that. At the same time, however, I want to suggest that furtive and sometimes effective ways of exercising freedom of assembly do happen in prison, and that we won't be able to conceptualize that form of resistance without conceding that point. The forms of solidarity and action that do emerge within prisons, including hunger strikes, also constitute a form of freedom of assembly, or a form of solidarity implied by such a freedom, and that also needs to be acknowledged as an active form of resistance. So already we see that the street and the square are not the only platforms for political resistance, and that where there is no freedom to enter the square or take to the street, grounds for resistance certainly exist. Can the four walls of the prison cell also turn out to be a platform, analogous perhaps to the overturned tank that suddenly becomes a platform on which people stand to voice their public opposition to the military, as happened in Cairo in 2009? The confined body does not always have the freedom to move, but can it still make use of its confinement to express resistance? At such moments, the public square is not the support for such action (though people gathered there, supporting those in prison, surely can be support, and can make use of that spatial support and its symbolic power), but support assumes yet another meaning, on the inside and the outside, in modes of solidarity, through ways that the body can exercise the refusal to eat and to work, to devise modes of communication, and to refuse to be a functional prisoner, intervening to thwart the reproduction of the institution of the prison. Prisons depend upon the successful regulation of human acts and movements, the reproduction of the body of the prisoner, and when that regulatory power fails, as it does, for instance, in the hunger strike, so too does the prison lose its capacity to function. Moreover, this failure to function is also linked to the imperiling or the killing of the prisoner itself. One might remember in Kafka's "In the Penal Colony" that the apparatus of punishment destroys the prisoner precisely when it goes out of control. This going out of control is perhaps induced by the hunger striker, but really, what is wanted is to expose the killing machine that the prison has always been, even when it works efficiently. For if the effective reproduction of the prisoner takes place in tandem with the decimation of the condition of livability for the prisoner, then death-bound movement is already happening prior to any hunger strike. The hunger strike exposes the death-dealing already at work in the prison. In this sense, the hunger strike is a bodily enactment, following its own protocols of performativity; it enacts what it seeks to show, and to resist.

Of course, each of these situations has to be considered in context. The recent assemblies on the street or in public squares, whether those of the Occupy movements or los Indignados in Spain, were concerned to provide provisional support for those assembled at the same time that they sought to facilitate broader demand for forms of enduring support under conditions in which more and more people were losing work, suffering salary cuts, and losing housing and public benefits. So the assembly does not exactly mirror the broader structure of the economic world. But certain principles get elaborated in those smaller assemblies that can nevertheless produce—or renew—ideals of equality and interdependency that may well be transposed onto larger national and global contexts. What the assembly does and what it says are linked together, though they are not always the same; the political demand is at once enacted and made, exemplified and communicated. All this means is that there is an invariably performative dimension to the kinds of demands that are made, where performativity functions as a chiastic relation between body and language. It is not, then, exclusively or primarily as subjects bearing abstract rights that we take to the streets. We take to the streets because we need to walk or move there; we need streets to be built so that, whether or not we are in a wheelchair, for instance, we can move there, and we can pass through that space without obstruction, harassment, administrative detention, or fear of injury or death. If we are on the streets, it is because we are bodies that require public forms of support to stand and move, and to live a life that matters (I take it that this broad claim from disability studies—that all bodies require support to move—has implications for thinking about what supports public mobilizations and, in particular, what supports mobilizations for public funding of infrastructural support). This vulnerability shows, whether or not we feel particularly vulnerable at the moment. Mobility is itself a right of the body, but it is also a precondition for the exercise of other rights, including the right of assembly itself. Many people are mobilizing around the right to walk, including the important Slut Walks that began to happen throughout the world as a way of embodying and refusing a label, and claiming the streets as a site that should be free of harassment and rape. Sometimes it is a perilous act to walk—to walk alone at night if you are a woman or trans— or to gather, even though police violence may be waiting. People are mobilizing around the rights of women to walk the street in religious garb, of trans women to walk to work or to march in acts of solidarity with other trans women or for broader social struggles. The right to walk on the street if you are black and it is night without someone assuming you are a criminal. The right of the disabled to walk, to have pavements and machines that make it possible. The right of a Palestinian to walk any street in Hebron, where apartheid rules prevail. Such rights should be common and unremarkable, and sometimes they are. But sometimes to walk the street, to exercise that small freedom, poses a challenge to a certain regime, a minor performative disruption enacted by a kind of motion that is at once a movement in that double sense, bodily and political.

That action, I would suggest, has to be supported through solidarity, to be sure, but also by infrastructural conditions, by law, and by the absence of violent or coercive efforts to thwart the way. The struggles I mentioned above presume that bodies have been constrained and are at risk of constraint, that they can be without work and without mobility, that they can suffer violence and forms of coercion. Am I trying to say that bodies are not active, but vulnerable? Or that even vulnerable bodies can act? My argument, in fact, is that it would be as mistaken to think of the body as primarily or definitionally active as it would be to think of the body as primarily and definitionally vulnerable and inactive. If we have to have a definition, it will depend, rather, on being able to think vulnerability and agency together. I am especially aware of how counterproductive it can be to understand women's bodies as particularly vulnerable. We immediately enter into uncertain terrain, given the long and lamentable gender politics that allocates the distinction between passive and active to women and men, respectively. Yet, if we say that certain groups are differentially vulnerable, we are only saying that under certain regimes of power, some groups are targeted more readily than others, some suffer poverty more than others, some are exposed to police violence more than others. We are making a sociological observation that would have to be backed up in one way or another. And yet, that sociological claim can very easily become a new norm of description, at which point women become defined by their vulnerability. At such a point, the very problem that the description is meant to address becomes reproduced and ratified by the very description.

This is one reason we have to pay attention to what it means to mobilize vulnerability, and what it means, more specifically, to mobilize vulnerability in concert. For many of us, that is, for many people, the moment of actively appearing on the street involves a deliberate risk of exposure. Perhaps the word "exposure" helps us think vulnerability outside the trap of ontology and foundationalism. This is especially true for those who, exposed, appear on the street without permits, who are opposing the police or the military or other security forces without weapons. Although one is shorn of protection, to be sure, one is not reduced to some sort of "bare life." There is no sovereign power jettisoning the subject outside the domain of the political as such; on the contrary, there is a more varied and diffuse operation of power and force that detains and encroaches on bodies in the street or in the cell or on the periphery of towns and borders—and this is a specifically political form of destitution.

Of course, feminist theorists have for a long time argued that women suffer social vulnerability disproportionately.[9] And though there is always a risk in claiming that women are especially vulnerable—given how many other groups are entitled to make the same claim, and given that the category of women is intersected by class, race, age, and a number of other vectors of power and sites of potential discrimination and injury—there is still something important to be taken from this tradition. The claim can sometimes be taken to mean that women have an unchanging and defining vulnerability, and that kind of argument makes the case for paternalistic provisions of protection. If women are regarded as especially vulnerable and seek protected status, it becomes the responsibility of the state or other paternal powers to provide that protection. According to that model, feminist activism not only petitions paternal authority for special dispensations and protections, but affirms that inequality of power that situates women in a powerless position and, by implication, men in a more powerful one. And where it does not simply or exclusively put "men" in the position of providing protection, it invests state structures with the paternalistic obligation to facilitate the achievement of feminist goals. Such a view is very different from one that claims, for instance, that women are at once vulnerable and capable of resistance, and that vulnerability and resistance can, and do, and even must happen at the same time, as we see in certain forms of feminist self-defense and institutions (battered women's shelters, for example) that seek to provide protection without enlarging paternalistic powers, and as happens through networks that support trans women in Turkey or anywhere the expanded and expandable category of women suffers harassment or injury by virtue of appearing as it does.

Of course, there are good reasons to argue for the differential vulnerability of women; they suffer disproportionately from poverty and illiteracy, two very important dimensions of any global analysis of women's conditions (and two reasons why none of us will be "postfeminist" until such time as these conditions are fully overcome). But many of the feminists who have made the turn to vulnerability, as it were, have done so in order to increase the protected standing of women in human rights organizations and international courts. This juridification of the feminist project seeks to prioritize the language needed to strengthen such an appeal to the courts. As important as such appeals may be, they provide a limited language for understanding feminist forms of resistance that are popular and extralegal, the dynamics of mass movements, civil society initiatives, and forms of political resistance informed and mobilized by vulnerability.

The need to establish a politics that avoids the retrenchment of paternalism seems clear. At the same time, if this resistance to paternalism objects to all state and economic institutions that provide social welfare, then the demand for infrastructural support becomes illegible within its terms, even self-defeating. Hence, this task is made all the more difficult under conditions of increasing precarity in which ever greater numbers of people are exposed to homelessness, unemployment, illiteracy, and inadequate health care. The struggle, in my view, is how to make the feminist claim effectively that such institutions are crucial to sustaining lives at the same time that feminists resist modes of paternalism that reinstate and naturalize relations of inequality.

So though the value of vulnerability has been important to feminist theory and politics, this does not mean that vulnerability serves as a defining characteristic of women as a group. I would oppose this effort to install a new norm for the category of women that rests on a foundational notion of vulnerability. Indeed, the very debate about who belongs to the group called "women" marks a distinct zone of vulnerability, namely, those who are non–gender conforming, and whose exposure to discrimination, harassment, and violence is clearly heightened on those grounds. So some provisionally bound group called "women" is neither more vulnerable than a provisionally bound group called "men" nor is it particularly useful or true to try to demonstrate that women value vulnerability more than men do. Rather, certain kinds of gender-defining attributes, like vulnerability and invulnerability, are distributed unequally under certain regimes of power, and precisely for the purpose of shoring up certain regimes of power that disenfranchise women. We think about goods as distributed unequally under capitalism as well as natural resources, especially water, but we should also surely consider that one way of managing populations is to distribute vulnerability unequally such that "vulnerable populations" are established within discourse and policy. More recently, we note that social movements and policy analysts refer to precarious populations, and that political strategies are accordingly devised to think about ameliorating conditions of precarity.[10] But this same demand is also made through broad popular struggles that both expose and mobilize precarity, showing, as it were, the possibilities of performative political action that emerge in the midst of precarity. It seems clear that if the designation of vulnerability or precarity effaces this form of political demand, it further entrenches the very condition from which it seeks alleviation.

So we see the risk of using the term "vulnerability" at all. But is there also a risk in shying away from the term? Does precarity give vulnerability a specifically political valence, and are we better off with one term or another? I am not sure we resolve the issue by changing terms, since both of them run certain kinds of risks.

There is of course an even more sinister way of wielding both categories of precarity and of vulnerability. Within the terms of both military and economic policy, certain populations are effectively targeted as injurable (with impunity) or disposable (living on in a disposable condition or no longer living, quite literally disposed of, a distinction that constitutes an interval in the time-space of social death). This kind of explicit or implicit marking is used to justify the infliction of injury upon such populations (as we see in times of war, or in state violence against undocumented

citizens). So "vulnerability" can be a way of targeting a population for decimation. This has produced a paradox within neoliberalism and its notion of "responsibilization" that designates such
populations as accountable for their own precarious position, or
their accelerated experience of precaritization. As a counter to this
nefarious form of moralizing, human rights advocates have defended the idea of vulnerability as they insist on the need for legal
and institutional protection for such groups. The notion of vulnerability here works in two ways, to target a population or to
protect it, which means that the term has been used to establish a
restrictive political logic according to which being targeted and
being protected are the only two alternatives. We can see that the
term, so deployed, effectively effaces both popular movements (if
not forms of popular sovereignty) and active struggles for resistance and social and political transformation. We may think that
these two ways of using the notion of vulnerability are antithet-
ical, and they are, but only within the terms of a problematic logic,
one that displaces some other forms of political rationality and
practice that are arguably more pressing and more promising.

So targeting and protecting are practices that belong to the same
rationale of power. If precarious populations have produced their
own situation, then they are not situated within a regime of power
that reproduces precarity in systemic ways. Their own actions,
or their own failures, are the cause of their precarious situations.
If they are seen as in need of protection, and if paternalistic forms
of power (which sometimes do include philanthropy and human-
itarian NGOs) seek to install themselves in permanent positions
of power to represent the powerless, then those very populations
are excluded from democratic processes and mobilizations. The
answer to this dilemma is neither to position precarious popula-

tions as hyperresponsible on a moral model nor, conversely, to position them as suffering populations in need of "care" by good Christians (as the social democratic discourse in France, with its implicit affiliation with Christian values, currently maintains).

This approach takes vulnerability and invulnerability as political effects, unequally distributed effects of a field of power that acts on and through bodies; these swift inversions show that vulnerability and invulnerability are not essential features of men or women, but, rather, processes of gender formation, the effects of modes of power that have as one of their aims the production of gender differences along lines of inequality. We can see evidence of this rationale when, for instance, masculinity is said to be "attacked" by feminism—in which case it is masculinity in the "vulnerable" position—or when the general public is said to be "attacked" by sexual and gender minorities of various kinds, or when the state of California is now understood to be "under attack" because it has lost its white majority, or when the state of Arizona is said to be "under attack" by its Latino population, and so trying to establish an ever more impermeable border to the south. Various European nationalities are now said to be "under attack" by new immigrant communities, at which point dominant groups and their racist representatives are construed as occupying a vulnerable condition.

This strategic use of vulnerability runs contrary to the kind of analysis derived from psychoanalytic feminism that goes something like this: the masculine position, construed in such a way, is effectively built through a denial of its own constitutive vulnerability. I believe we all probably know one version of this argument or another.[11] This denial or disavowal requires the political institution of denial, projection, and displacement. It gathers round the sign of the feminine. But that analysis has to confront an inversion of its formulation. After all, the production of a hypervulnerability (of the nation, of masculinity) sometimes establishes a rationale for the containment of both women and minorities. The one who achieves this impermeability erases—that is, expunges and externalizes—all trace of a memory of vulnerability, effectively seeking to control contemporary feelings of unmanageable vulnerability. The person who considers himself, by definition, to be invulnerable effectively says, "I was never vulnerable, and if I was, it wasn't true, and I have no memory of that condition, and it certainly is not true now"—the discourse attests to what it denies. An ever proliferating set of statements is belied by the bodily condition of their very enunciation, showing something of the political syntax of disavowal. Yet, it also tells us something about how histories can be told in order to support an ideal of the self one wishes were true; such histories depend on disavowal for their coherence, a coherence that is especially brittle.

Although psychoanalytic perspectives such as these are important as a way of gaining insight into this particular way that vulnerability is distributed along gender lines, they only go part of the way toward the kind of analysis needed here, since if we say that some person or some group denies vulnerability, we are assuming not only that the vulnerability was already there, but also that it is in some sense undeniable. Denial is always an effort to deflect from what is obstinately the case, so the potential refutation of denial is part of its very definition. In this sense, although the denial of vulnerability is impossible, it happens all the time. Of course, one cannot make an easy analogy between individual and group formations, and yet modes of denial or disavowal can be seen to traverse them both. For instance, to certain defenders of the military rationale for the destruction of targeted groups or populations, we might say, "you act as if you yourself were not vulnerable to the kind of destruction you cause." Or to defenders of certain forms of neoliberal economics, "you act as if you yourself could never belong to a population whose work and life are precarious, who can suddenly be deprived of basic rights or access to housing or health care, or who lives with anxiety about how and whether work will ever arrive." In this way, then, we assume that those who seek to expose others to a vulnerable position—or to install them there—as well as those who seek to posit and maintain a position of invulnerability for themselves all seek to deny a vulnerability by virtue of which they are obstinately, if not unbearably, bound to the others they seek to subjugate. If one is tied to another against one's will, even when, precisely when, a contract is the means of subjugation, the tie can be quite literally maddening, a form of unacceptably enforced dependency, as happens in slave labor and other forms of coercive contract. The problem is not dependency as such, but its tactical exploitation. And this then opens up the question of what it would mean to separate dependency from exploitation, so that the one does not immediately mean the other. Forms of political resistance that champion forms of autonomy freed of all dependency perhaps make this mistake of understanding dependency as exploitation. Of course, as Albert Memmi pointed out in his important text, *Dependence,* the term has been used to rationalize forms of colonial power, suggesting that some populations are more dependent than others, that they require colonial rule, that that is the only way to bring them, or some of them, into modernity and civilization.[12] But shall we then let that term remain tainted in that way, and is there another way to mobilize that term, even forcing a certain break with its legacy?

How else would we understand the general claim that bodies invariably depend on enduring social relations and institutions for their survival and flourishing? If we make such a claim, are we not precisely saying what bodies finally are, or offering a general ontology of the body? And attributing a general primacy to vulnerability? On the contrary: precisely because bodies are formed and sustained in relation to infrastructural supports (or their absence) and social and technological networks or webs of relation, we cannot extract the body from its constituting relations—and those relations are always economically and historically specific. So if we say that the body is vulnerable, we are saying that the body is vulnerable to economics and to history. This means that vulnerability always takes an object, is always formed and lived in relation to a set of conditions that are outside, yet part of, the body itself. We could say that the body exists then in an ecstatic relation to the supporting conditions it has or must demand, but this means that the body never exists in an ontological mode that is distinct from its historical situation. Perhaps it helps to put it this way: the body is exposed, to history, to precarity, and to force, but also to what is unbidden and felicitous, like passion and love, or sudden friendship or sudden or unexpected loss. Indeed, everything unexpected about loss might be said to touch upon a vulnerability that we have that we cannot predict or control in advance. In that sense, vulnerability denotes some dimension of what cannot be foreseen or predicted or controlled in advance, and that might be the stray comment that comes your way by someone who happens to be riding the same bus as you, or the sudden loss of friendship, or the brutal obliteration of a life by bombing. These are not the same, but as creatures who are open to what happens, we can perhaps be said to be vulnerable to what happens when what happens is not always knowable in advance. Vulnerability implicates us in what is beyond us yet part of us, constituting one central dimension of what might tentatively be called our embodiment.

Perhaps now I can make clear several points about vulnerability that seek neither to idealize nor to discount its political importance. The first is that vulnerability cannot be associated exclusively with injurability. All responsiveness to what happens is a function and effect of vulnerability—of being open to a history, registering an impression, or having something impressed upon one's understanding. Vulnerability may be a function of openness, that is, of being open to a world that is not fully known or predictable. Part of what a body does (to use the phrase of Deleuze, derived from his reading of Spinoza) is to open onto the body of another, or a set of others, and for this reason bodies are not self-enclosed kinds of entities.[13] They are always in some sense outside themselves, exploring or navigating their environment, extended and even sometimes dispossessed through the senses.[14] If we can become lost in another, or if our tactile, motile, haptic, visual, olfactory, or auditory capacities comport us beyond ourselves, that is because the body does not stay in its own place, and because dispossession of this kind characterizes bodily sense more generally.

It is also why it is important to speak sometimes about the regulation of the senses as a political matter—there are certain photographs of the injury or destruction of bodies in war, for example, that we are often forbidden to see precisely because there is a fear that this body will feel something about what those other bodies underwent, or that this body, in its sensory comportment outside itself, will not remain enclosed, monadic, and individual. Indeed, we might ask what kind of regulation of the senses— those modes of ecstatic relationality—might have to be instituted for individualism to be maintained as an ontology required for both economics and politics.

Although we often speak as if vulnerability is a contingent and passing circumstance, there are reasons not to accept that as a general view. Of course, it is always possible to say, "I was vulnerable then, but I am not vulnerable anymore," and we say that in relation to specific situations in which we felt ourselves to be at risk or injurable. Those can be economic or financial situations when we feel that we are exploited, having lost work, or find ourselves in conditions of poverty, in need of public assistance that is itself being cut back assiduously. Or they can be emotional situations in which we are very much vulnerable to rejection, but later find that we have lost that vulnerability. Even as it makes sense that we speak this way, it makes equal sense to treat with caution the seductions of ordinary discourse at this moment. And though we may legitimately feel that we are vulnerable in some instances and not in others, the condition of our vulnerability is itself not changeable. This does not mean that we are objectively or subjectively equally vulnerable all the time. But it does mean that it is a more or less implicit or explicit feature of our experience. To say that any of us are vulnerable beings is to mark our radical dependency not only on others, but on a sustaining and sustainable world. This has implications for understanding who we are as emotionally and sexually passionate beings, as bound up with others from the start, but also as beings who seek to persist, and whose persistence can be imperiled or sustained depending on whether social, economic, and political structures offer sufficient support for a livable life.

Populations marked by differential vulnerability and precarity are not for that reason immobilized. When political struggles emerge to oppose such conditions, they are mobilizing precarity, and even sometimes quite deliberately mobilizing the public exposure of the body, even when it means being exposed to force or detention or possibly death. It is not that vulnerability is converted into resistance, at which point strength triumphs over vulnerability. Strength is not quite the opposite of vulnerability, and this becomes clear, I would suggest, when vulnerability is itself mobilized, not as an individual strategy, but in concert. This is probably not what Hannah Arendt had in mind when she said that politics depends on acting in concert—I can't imagine she would have much liked the Slut Walks.[15] But perhaps if we rethink her view so that the body, and its requirements, becomes part of the action and aim of the political, we can start to approach a notion of plurality that is thought together with both performativity and interdependency.

Now, I realize that I have introduced new terms without being able to clarify my meaning sufficiently. "Interdependency" is one. I'd caution in this way: We cannot presume that interdependency is some beautiful state of coexistence; it is not the same as social harmony. Inevitably, we rail against those on whom we are most dependent (or those who are most dependent on us), and there is no way to dissociate dependency from aggression once and for all—this was perhaps the profound insight of Melanie Klein, but surely also Thomas Hobbes in another idiom. In the early 1980s, the black American feminist Bernice Johnson Reagon put the point this way: "I feel as if I'm gonna keel over any minute and die. That is often what it feels like if you're really doing coalition work. Most of the time you feel threatened to the core and if you don't, you're not really doing no coalescing. . . . You don't go into coalition because you just like it. The only reason you would consider trying to team up with somebody who could possibly kill you, is because that's the only way you can figure you can stay alive." Toward the end of her remarks, she makes clear that interdependency includes the threat of death: about the idea of a common world, one we could call "our common world," she remarks, "You must be sure you understand that you ain't gonna be able to have an 'our' [as in our world] that don't include Bernice Johnson Reagon, cause I don't plan to go nowhere! That's why we have to have coalitions. Cause I ain't gonna let you live unless you let me live. Now there's danger in that, but there's also the possibility that we can both live—if you can stand it."[16]

In a sense, the people you find in the street or off the street or in the prison or on the periphery, on the path that still is no street, or in whatever basement that houses the coalition that is possible at the moment are not precisely the ones you chose. I mean, for the most part, when we arrive, we do not know who else is arriving, which means that we accept a kind of unchosen dimension to our solidarity with others. Perhaps we could say that the body is always exposed to people and impressions it does not have a say about, does not get to predict or fully control, and that these conditions of social embodiment are those we have not fully brokered. I want to suggest that solidarity emerges from this rather than from deliberate agreements we enter knowingly.

Finally, then, how do we understand resistance as the mobilization of vulnerability or exposure? Let me just offer the following as a way to close: When the bodies of those deemed "disposable" or "ungrievable" assemble in public view (as happens time and again when the undocumented arrive in the streets in the United States as part of public demonstrations), they are saying, "we have not slipped quietly into the shadows of public life: we have not become the glaring absence that structures your public life." In a way, the collective assembling of bodies is an exercise of the popular will, a taking up or taking over of a street that seems to belong to another public, a gathering up of the pavement for the purposes of action and speech that press up against the limits of social recognizability. But the streets and the square are not the only way that people assemble, and we know that social networking produces links of solidarity that can be quite impressive and effective in the virtual domain.

Whether bodies appear in public shorn of technology or hold cell phones up in concert (as many now do to document police violence in demonstrations), or whether bodies are interned under forcible conditions of isolation and destitution, the body remains a resource, not an endless or a magical one. A group acting together has to be supported to act, and this takes on special meaning when the action takes place increasingly as a way of demanding enduring support and the conditions of livable life. It could sound like a vicious circle, but it should come as no surprise that the bodies gathered in social movements are asserting the social modality of the body. This can be a minor way to enact the world we wish to see, or to refuse the one that is doing us in. Is this not a form of deliberate exposure and persistence, the embodied demand for a livable life that shows us the simultaneity of being precarious and acting?

Chapter 5

"We the People"—Thoughts on Freedom of Assembly

"We the People" is a phrase in the Preamble to the U.S. Constitution that is said to have initiated the legal break from Britain by the United States, but it is also a phrase that is implicitly invoked in any number of public assemblies that do not share the legal framework of the United States—Etienne Balibar's title *We, the People of Europe?* is a case in point. In fact, it is rare that such a phrase is actually spoken or written, and yet, does its performative force get communicated by other means? I take my point of departure in this chapter not only from the Occupy movements, but from other kinds of assemblies that are appearing precisely as public space is either sold off or subject to various kinds of securitarian control, as well as from the public education movements in Chile, Montreal, and throughout Europe as students object to new budget cuts and the standardization of the excellence protocols. I don't mean to suggest that all of these assemblies are the same, or that they enunciate perfectly parallel structures.

Through what means is the claim to public space being made? If it is not always language that names and forms the people as a unity, is it perhaps taking place with other bodily resources—through silence, concerted movement, stillness, and that persistent clustering of bodies in public space throughout the day and night that has characterized the Occupy Movement? Perhaps these recent assemblies prompt us to ask whether we need to revise our ideas of public space in order to take account of the forms of alliance and solidarity that are only partially dependent on the ability to appear in the public square. That was, of course, Arendt's famous claim, that politics not only requires a space of appearance, but bodies that do appear. For her, appearing was a precondition of speaking, and only public speech really counted as action. In revolutions, she told us, there is a certain acting in concert, or plural action. But could she allow the plural movement of bodies to articulate the "we," that plurality considered so essential to democracy? How would we understand public assembly as a political enactment that is distinct from speech?

There are many examples of people coming together, forming a way of speaking as a collective, and demanding a change in policy, exposing the absence of state legitimacy or the dissolution of a government. Although Tahrir Square seemed for a time to be emblematic of the democratic power of public assemblies, we have seen how counterrevolutions deploy their own ideas of who "the people" are, even if they bring on police and military authorities that attack and imprison the people. So if we let this developing example guide our thinking, then no one popular assembly comes to represent the entirety of the people, but each positing of the people through assembly risks or invites a set of conflicts that, in turn, prompt a growing set of doubts about who the people really are. After all, let us assume that no *one* assembly can rightly become the basis for generalizations about *all* assemblies, and that the efforts to associate a particular uprising or mobilization with democracy itself is a temptation as thrilling as it is erroneous—it cuts short the conflictual process through which the idea of the people is articulated and negotiated. In some ways, the problem is epistemological: Can we ever really know who the "we" is who assembles in the street, and whether any given assembly really represents the people as such? And whether any given assembly can represent what we mean by freedom of assembly as such? Every example fails, and yet certain themes tend to recur such that we can reapproach the way the claim of "we the people" is made. Sometimes it is quite explicitly a battle over words, political signifiers, or images and descriptions. But prior to any group starting to debate that language, there is a coming together of bodies that speaks, as it were, in another way. Assemblies assert and enact themselves by speech or silence, by action or steady inaction, by gesture, by gathering together as a group of bodies in public space, organized by the infrastructure—visible, audible, tangible, exposed in ways both deliberate and unwilled, interdependent in forms both organized and spontaneous.

So let us assume from the start that it is not by way of a particular and punctual speech act that a group comes together as a "people." Although we often think that the declarative speech act by which "we the people" consolidates its popular sovereignty is one that issues from such an assembly, it is perhaps more appropriate to say that *the assembly is already speaking before it utters any words,* that by coming together it is *already* an enactment of a popular will; that enactment signifies quite differently from the way a single and unified subject declares its will through a vocalized proposition. The "we" voiced in language is already enacted by the gathering of bodies, their gestures and movements, their vocalizations, and their ways of acting in concert. To act in concert does not mean to act in conformity; it may be that people are moving or speaking in several different directions at once, even at cross-purposes. And it does not mean they speak the exact same words, though sometimes that happens in a chant or in a verbal relay as in Occupy public assemblies. And sometimes "the people" act by way of their collective silence or their ironic use of language; their humor and even their mockery take up and take over a language they seek to derail from its usual ends.

Already there are two points I want to underscore: The first is that the actions by which people assemble and assert themselves to be a people may be spoken or enacted in another way. The second is that we have to be able to think of such acts as plural action, presupposing a plurality of bodies who enact their convergent and divergent purposes in ways that fail to conform to a single kind of acting, or reduce to a single kind of claim. At issue for us will be the question of how politics changes when the idea of abstract rights vocally claimed by individuals gives way to a plurality of embodied actors who enact their claims, sometimes through language, sometimes not. Let us consider then how we might, in light of this shift in framework, understand freedom of assembly. In what sense is it a right, and how is it claimed? As a right, what does it presuppose about who we are and who we might be? The right to exercise the freedom of assembly is by now well documented in international law. The International Labour Organization makes explicit that rights to assembly (or associational rights) are tied to the rights of collective bargaining.[1] This means that people assemble in order to negotiate the conditions of work, including demands for safety, job security, and protection against exploitation, but also the right to collective bargaining itself. The right assembles workers together—no one has a right of assembly without a group of others who are in a structurally similar position in relation to the workforce.

In some human rights discourses, the freedom of assembly is described as a fundamental form of freedom that deserves to be protected by government, which means that governments are obligated to protect that freedom; paradoxically, governments must protect the freedom of assembly against governmental interference, which is a way of saying that governments are under strict obligations to restrain themselves from attacking the rights of assembly by the illegitimate use of police and judicial powers to detain, arrest, harass, threaten, censor, imprison, injure, or kill. As we can see, there is a risk in this formulation from the start: Does freedom of assembly depend upon being protected *by* government, or does it depend upon a protection *from* government? And does it make sense for the people to rely on government to protect itself from government? Does the right only exist if a government confers this right on its people, and does it only exist to the extent that a government agrees to protect that right? If so, then the destruction of those rights of assembly by a government cannot be opposed by asserting the rights of assembly. We can agree that freedom of assembly cannot be found in natural law, but is it still in some important way independent of any and every government? Does freedom of expression, in fact, exceed, even defy, those acts of government by which it is protected and/or violated? These rights do not, and cannot, depend on governmental protection in those cases when the legitimacy of a government and the power of the state are being contested precisely by such an assembly, or when a specific state has contravened the rights of assembly such that its population can no longer freely congregate without threat of state interference, including military and police brutality. Moreover, when the power of the state to "protect" rights is identical to the power of the state to withdraw that very protection, and people exercise the freedom of assembly to contest that form of arbitrary and illegitimate power that bestows and withdraws protection at will, then something in or of freedom of assembly moves outside the jurisdiction of state sovereignty. One aspect of state sovereignty is this very capacity to withdraw protection of the rights of populations.[2] That may be true, but perhaps what is being opposed is the idea that freedom of assembly itself can be lost as a right when the state opposes the aims of that assembly and seeks to outlaw assembly itself. That happens, as we know, when the state itself becomes engaged in facilitating the expansion of markets, in turning its own services over to financial institutions, and thereby transforming public entitlements into consumer goods or investment opportunities. The antiprivatization movement seeks to stop the saturation of the state in market forces. Such movements often happen in tandem with a call to question the legitimacy of a government that has assumed authoritarian powers—no one is arguing that free markets now foster democracy, as Milton Friedman notoriously did in Chile under Pinochet. In those cases in which privatization and authoritarianism are publicly opposed, the state uses its own military, police, and legal powers to suppress the freedom of assembly and other such (potentially revolutionary) freedoms.

So, freedom of assembly is something other than a specific right allocated and protected by existing nation-states. This is why, although there are many excellent studies on the history of freedom of assembly in the United States, for instance, they do not always give us insight into transnational forms of alliances, or global networks such as those that characterized the Occupy Movement. If we restrict the analysis of freedom of assembly to a particular national history of that right, we may unwittingly imply that the right only exists insofar as the state confers and protects that right. We may then depend upon the continuation of the nation-state to secure the efficacy of that right. That, of course, turns out not to be true if, by "freedom of assembly," the nation-state protects precisely that right that could, if collectively exercised, bring down the state itself. I take it that this is what is meant when Arendt and others see in freedom of assembly a recurrence of the right of revolution.[3] Still, even if a particular regime contains or protects such a right, it seems to me that the freedom of assembly has to precede and exceed any form of government that confers and protects that right of assembly. I say this not to affirm forms of permanent anarchy, and certainly not to condone forms of mob rule, but only to suggest that freedom of assembly may well be a precondition of politics itself, one that presumes that bodies can move and gather in an unregulated way, enacting their political demands in a space that, as a result, becomes public, or redefines an existing understanding of the public.

That assembly may be called "the people" or it may be one version of "the people"—they do not speak in one voice or even in one language. But they are beings with the capacity to move with whatever technical and infrastructural supports they require to do so (this is, importantly, an insight from disability studies that has concrete implications for thinking through public assembly). And that means that they can resolve to stand still, not to move, even to become immoveable in their desires and their demands. The power to move or be still, to speak and to act, belongs to the assembly prior to, and in excess of, whatever rights a particular government decides to confer or to protect. The coming together of a crowd has, as John Inazu contends, "an expressive function" prior to any particular claim or utterance it may make.[4] That very power of government may well become what freedom of assembly opposes, and at that moment, we see the operation of a form of popular sovereignty that is distinct from state sovereignty, and whose task it is to distinguish itself from the latter.

How, then, do we think about the freedom of assembly and *popular* sovereignty? I know that some people have come to consider "sovereignty" a bad word, one that associates politics with a singular subject and a form of executive power with territorial claims. Sometimes it is used as synonymous with mastery, and other times with subordination. Perhaps it carries other connotations, though, that we would not want to lose altogether. One only needs to consider debates about native sovereignty in Canada or read the important work of J. Kēhaulani Kauanui on the paradoxes of Hawaiian sovereignty to see how crucial this notion can be for popular mobilizations.[5] Sovereignty can be one way of describing acts of political self-determination, which is why popular movements of indigenous people struggling for sovereignty have become important ways to lay claim to space, to move freely, to express one's views, and to seek reparation and justice. Although elections are the way that government officials are supposed to represent popular sovereignty (or the "popular will" more specifically), the meaning of popular sovereignty has never been fully exhausted by the act of voting. Of course, voting is essential for any concept of popular sovereignty, but the exercise of sovereignty neither begins nor ends with the act of voting. As democratic theorists have argued for some time, elections do not fully transfer sovereignty from the populace to its elected representatives—something of popular sovereignty always remains nontransferable, marking the outside of the electoral process. If not, there would be no popular means of objecting to corrupt electoral processes. In a sense, the power of the populace remains separate from the power of those elected, even after they have elected them, for only in its separateness can it continue to contest the conditions and results of elections as well as the actions of elected officials. If the sovereignty of the people is fully transferred to, and replaced by, those whom the majority elect, then what is lost are those powers we call critical, those actions we call resistance, and that lived possibility we call revolution.

So "popular sovereignty" certainly translates into electoral power when the people vote, but that is never a full or adequate translation. Something of popular sovereignty remains untranslatable, nontransferable, and even unsubstitutable, which is why it can both elect and dissolve regimes. As much as popular sovereignty legitimates parliamentary forms of power, it also retains the power to withdraw its support from those same forms when they prove to be illegitimate. If parliamentary forms of power require popular sovereignty for their very legitimacy, they also surely fear it, for there is something about popular sovereignty that runs counter to, and exceeds or outruns, every parliamentary form that it institutes and grounds. An elected regime can be brought to a halt or overcome by that assembly of people who speak "in the name of the people," enacting the very "we" that holds final legitimating power under conditions of democratic rule. In other words, the conditions of democratic rule depend finally on an exercise of popular sovereignty that is never fully contained or expressed by any particular democratic order, but which is the condition of its democratic character. This is an extraparliamentary power without which no parliament can function legitimately, and that threatens every parliament with dysfunction or even dissolution. We may again want to call it an "anarchist" interval or a permanent principle of revolution that resides within democratic orders, one that shows up more or less both at moments of founding and moments of dissolution, but is also operative in the freedom of assembly itself.

Enactments, I would like to suggest, are not fully reducible to assertions; rather, assertions are but one form of political enactment, which is why the sphere of political performativity includes and exceeds verbal and written utterances. In this way, I seek to draw upon Jason Frank's important formulation of "constituent moments" in which the enactment of the people exceeds its representation; in his view, the people must be enacted to be represented, and yet no enactment can succeed in representing them.[6] In his view, this dissonance between enactment and representation proves to be a core paradox of democratic assemblies.

As long as the state controls the very conditions of freedom of assembly, popular sovereignty becomes an instrument of state sovereignty, and the legitimating conditions of the state are lost at the same time that the freedom of assembly has been robbed of both its critical and its democratic functions. I would add here that if we assume that popular sovereignty depends on state sovereignty, and we think that the sovereign state maintains control, through its power to make an exception, over which part of the population will be protected by the law and which will not, then we have, unwittingly perhaps, reduced that power of popular sovereignty to bare life, or to a form of anarchism that presupposes a break with state sovereignty. But if that break is already there within popular sovereignty or if popular sovereignty is that break, then the reduction of popular sovereignty to state sovereignty covers over and displaces that most important potential, one that a large number of popular movements struggling for self-determination affirm as their ultimate organizing value. The invocation of the people becomes—and must become—contestable at the very moment that it appears. "Appearance" can designate visible presence, spoken words, but also networked representation and silence. Moreover, we have to be able to think of such acts as plural action, presupposing a plurality of bodies who enact their convergent purpose in ways that do not require strict conformity to a single kind of acting, or to a single kind of claim, and who do not together constitute a single kind of subject.

Even if all this seems clear enough, a difficult and persistent question remains: Who are "the people"? Have we yet posed that question? I am aware that this topic has been amply discussed by Jacques Derrida, Bonnie Honig, Etienne Balibar, Ernesto Laclau, and Jacques Rancière, and I don't purport to add anything new to those debates at this time. But each of them accepts the point that any designation of "the people" works through delimiting a boundary that sets up terms of inclusion and exclusion. That is one reason why democratic theorists have sought to underscore the temporal and open-ended character of "the people," often seeking to incorporate a check on the exclusionary logic by which any designation proceeds. We have heard as well about the imaginary character of "the people," suggesting that any reference to the term risks a certain nationalism or utopianism, or that this makes "the people" into an indispensable empty signifier.[7] For the moment, I want only to underscore that we cannot simply rely on a snapshot to confirm the number of bodies that constitute who the people are. We cannot simply turn to aerial photographs taken by police charged with managing crowds on the street to find out what the people want, or whether they really want it. Such a procedure would paradoxically rely on a technology that is meant to control populations, and that would make "the people" into an effect of demographic forensics. Any photograph, or any series of images, would doubtless have a frame or set of frames, and those frames would function as a potentially exclusionary designation, including what it captures by establishing a zone of the uncapturable. The same would be true of any video that starts and ends somewhere, composing a sequence. It would always be limited by the perspective by which its object is selectively crafted and conveyed.

One reason this point about visual representation is important is that no picture of the crowd can represent the people when not all the people have the power to assemble in the street, or at least not on the same street. Zooming in and zooming out will not help us here, since those are precisely ways of editing and selecting what and who will count, which means that we cannot separate the question of who the people are from the technology that establishes which people will count as the people. Perhaps "the people" is that designation that exceeds any and every visual frame that seeks to capture the people, and the more democratic frames are those that are able to orchestrate their porous character, where the frame does not immediately reproduce the strategy of containment, where the frame partially wrecks itself.

Sometimes the people, or some people, are confined or absent, or outside the purview of the street and the camera—they are the uncapturable, though they may well be captured in another sense. It never really happens that all of the possible people who are represented by the notion of "the people" show up in the same space and at the same time to claim that they are the people! As if they were all free to move, as if they all of their own volition arrived together in some space and time that can be described or photographed in some all-inclusive way!

Indeed, it would be odd, if not terrifying, to imagine every member of the group called "the people" coming together and speaking in unison—that would be a fantasy, if not a potentially persecutory phantasm, whose seductive power is linked with its fundamental unrealizability. Usually, we associate the event of everyone speaking the same thing at the same time with forms of fascism or other compulsory forms of conformity. In fact, "we the people"—the utterance, the chant, the written line—is always missing some group of people it claims to represent. Some people fail to show up or are constrained from doing so; many live on the margins of the metropole, some are congregated on the border in refugee camps waiting for documentation, transfer, and shelter, and yet others are in prison or detained in camps. Those who are situated elsewhere may, if they can, be saying something else, or they are texting or blogging, or functioning through new media; some are emphatically or indifferently not speaking at all. This means that "the people" never really arrive as a collective presence that speaks as a verbal chorus; whoever the people may be, they are surely internally divided, appearing differentially, sequentially, not at all, or in degree, probably also in some measure both gathered and dispersed, and so ultimately *not* a unity.[8] In fact, as we know from the summer demonstrations in both Turkey and Egypt in 2013, one group gathers in one place and claims to be the people, and another group gathers across the way and makes the same claim, or the government gathers a group of people precisely in order to take the image that functions as the visual signifier of "the people."

Access to any public square presupposes access to some media that relays the events outside of that space and time; the public square is now partially established as a media effect, but also as part of the enunciatory apparatus by which a group of people claims to be the people; the connection of the public square with the media that circulates the event means that the people disperse as they gather; the media image shows and disperses the gathering. This implies the need to radically rethink the public square as always already dispersed through the media representation without which it loses its representative claim. It also means that whoever the people may be is not quite known or knowable, and not only because the media frame limits and morphs the idea of the people it relays. What is known, however, is that the people, whoever they may be, show up and do not, are subject to various restrictions of movement and assembly, and are internally divided about who they are. Showing up together does not mean that everyone agrees with everything that is said in the name of the assembly or even that the assembly has a name. The contest over the name becomes a hegemonic struggle, and "the people" seems to be another name for that contest.

So, what follows? A people do not need to be united on every issue, and cannot be. And neither do they all have to gather in a single space for concerted action to take place *in the name of* the people. That name, "the people," even the declaration, "we the people," does not quite capture what the people do, for there is always something other than the particular group that has formed and appeared and seems to be speaking of what all the people might want, precisely because there is a gap between what happens in the name of the people and what the people want. Not all the people want the same thing or want it in the same way—this failure does not need to be lamented. The name of the people is appropriated, contested, and renewed, always at risk of being expropriated or dismissed, and the fragility and ferocity that mark the hegemonic struggle over the name are but signs of its democratic operation. So even as some speaker or set of speakers invoke a "we" that fairly and fully represents all the people, the plural "we" cannot really do what it nevertheless does; such speakers may surely continue to strive for more inclusive aims, underscoring the aspirational character of the "we," but if the "we" is to work politically, it has to be restricted to those who attempt to achieve and exercise hegemonic power through its invocation. Indeed, those who assemble as the "we," presenting themselves as "the people," are not finally *representing* the people fully and adequately; rather, they are performing several functions at once: for instance, if they can vote, they provide the legitimating ground for those who come to represent the people through elections. But perhaps equally importantly, the claim of elected officials to be representative requires the condensation of the people into a set of votes that can be tallied as a majority. In this sense, the people are abbreviated and nearly lost at the moment in which they elect those who represent them, and political representation in this sense abbreviates, quantifies, something we might call the will of the people. At the same time, something nonelectoral is also at work. The people who speak the "we," whether within the electoral process, outside it, or against it, constitute themselves as the people in the course of enacting or vocalizing that plural pronoun either literally or figuratively. Standing together in the face of the police can be precisely an enactment of that plural pronoun without saying a word. When the Turkish government in the summer of 2013 banned assemblies in Taksim Square, one man stood alone, facing the police, clearly "obeying" the law not to assemble. As he stood there, more individuals stood "alone" in proximity to him, but not exactly as a "crowd." They were standing as single individuals, but they were all standing, silent and motionless, as single individuals, evading the standard idea of an "assembly" yet producing another one in its place. They technically obeyed the law forbidding groups from assembling and moving by standing separately and saying nothing. This became an articulate yet wordless demonstration.[9]

THESE ACTS OF SELF-MAKING or self-constitution are not the same as representing a people who are already fully formed. The term "the people" does not only represent a preexisting collection of people; if it did, the term would postdate the production of the collectivity itself. Indeed, the term can never adequately represent a collectivity that is in the process of being made or making itself—both its inadequacy and its self-division are part of its enacted meaning and promise. The discursive invocation of the "we" refers then to a people whose needs, desires, and demands are not yet fully known, and whose coming together is bound up with a future that is yet to be lived out. Indeed, such practices of self-determination are not quite the same as acts of self-representation, and yet both of these are at work in exercising the freedom of assembly in which "we the people" is spoken or enacted in some way. That enactment is performative inasmuch as it brings into being the people whom it names, or it calls upon them to gather under the utterance. And this means that performative actions such as these are part of the process called political self-determination, designations of who we are that are also, at the same time, engaged in making that very "we." Further, the invocation of "we" separates popular sovereignty from state sovereignty; it names and inaugurates that separation time and again. The plurality always breaks with those who are elected, or whose election is questionable to us, or in relation to a state whose representatives we have never had the choice to elect, as is the clear case under occupation and for the undocumented and the partial or noncitizen.

So, something that must fail as representation, and that we might call nonrepresentational and nonrepresentative, nearly tautological, becomes the basis of democratic forms of political self-determination—popular sovereignty, distinct from state sovereignty, or, rather, popular sovereignty precisely as it intermittently distinguishes itself from state sovereignty. Popular sovereignty makes sense only in this perpetual act of separating from state sovereignty; thus, it is a way of *forming* a people through acts of self-designation and self-gathering; these are repeated enactments verbal and nonverbal, bodily and virtual, undertaken across different spatial and temporal zones, and on different kinds of public stages, virtual realities, and shadow regions. The vocalized performative, "we the people," is surely part of the enactment we are calling self-constitution, but this figure cannot be taken as a literal account of how political self-determination works. Not every act of political self-determination can be translated into that verbal utterance—such a move would make the verbal domain more privileged than any other. In fact, the enactment of political self-determination is necessarily a crossing of the linguistic and the bodily, even if the action is silent and the body is sequestered.

How do we, for instance, understand the hunger strike if not precisely as the practiced refusal of a body that cannot appear in public?[10] This means that appearing in public in a bodily form is not an adequate figure for political self-determination. At the same time, the hunger strike that is not reported and represented in public space fails to convey the power of the act itself. Prisoner networks are precisely those forms of solidarity that do not, cannot, appear in public in a bodily form, relying predominantly on digital media reports with few, if any, images. Those networks of prisoners, activists, lawyers, and extended kin and social relations, whether in Turkey, in Palestinian prisons and detention camps, or at Pelican Bay in California, are also forms of "assembly" in which those with suspended citizenship exercise a form of freedom through strikes, petitions, and forms of legal and political representation. Even as they do not appear, are not allowed to appear, they are nevertheless exercising a certain right to appear in public, either before the law or in public space, objecting precisely to the interdiction against appearing in public that is the condition of imprisonment.

Given all this, let us recapitulate what this means and does not mean for rethinking the freedom of assembly in relation to popular sovereignty: (1) popular sovereignty is thus a form of reflexive self-making that is separate from the very representative regime it legitimates; (2) it arises in the course of that very separation; (3) it cannot legitimate any particular regime without being separate from it, that is, partially uncontrolled by a regime and not operationalized as its instrument, and yet it is the basis from which legitimate government is formed through fair and inclusive elections; and (4) its act of self-making is actually a series of spatially distributed acts, ones that do not always operate in the same way and for the same purposes. Among the most important of these spatial distinctions is that between the public sphere and spheres of forcible confinement, including the prison where political prisoners, those who have exercised freedom of assembly and freedom of speech, are contained and subjugated. The passage into and out of the public sphere is regulated precisely by legal and police power and the institution of the prison. Further, (5) the enactment of "we the people" may or may not take linguistic form; speech and silence, movement and immobility, are all political enactments; the hunger strike is precisely the inverse of the fed body standing freely in the public domain and speaking—it marks and resists the deprivation of that right, and it enacts and exposes the deprivation that prison populations undergo.

The invocation of the people becomes—and must become—contestable at the very moment that it appears. "Appearance" can designate visible presence, spoken words, but also networked representation and concerted acts of silence. A differential form of power that takes both spatial and temporal forms establishes who may be part of such an enactment and the means and methods of such enactments. Confinement implies being spatially separated from public assemblies, but also involves the duration of the sentence, or the unknowable duration of indefinite detention. Since the public sphere is constituted in part through sites of forcible sequestering, the borders that define the public are also those that define the confined, the sequestered, the imprisoned, the expelled, and the disappeared. Whether we are speaking about the borders of the nation-state where the undocumented are confined within refugee encampments, where rights of citizenship are denied or indefinitely suspended, or about prisons where indefinite detention has become the norm, the interdiction against appearing, moving, and speaking in public becomes the precondition of embodied life. The prison is not exactly the inverse of the public sphere, since prisoner advocacy networks traverse the walls of the prison. Forms of prisoner resistance are forms of enactment that by definition cannot be part of the public square, though through networks of communication and proxy representation, they surely can. And yet, no matter how virtual we want to think the public sphere (and there are many good reasons for thinking that), the prison remains the limit case of the public sphere, marking the power of the state to control who can pass into the public and who must pass out of it. Thus, the prison is the limit case of the public sphere, and that freedom of assembly is haunted by the possibility of imprisonment. One may be imprisoned for what one says or one may be imprisoned simply for assembling. Or one may be imprisoned for writing or teaching about assemblies or about freedom struggles, or for teaching about popular struggles for sovereignty, such as teaching about the Kurdish freedom movement in Turkish universities.

All of these are reasons why those with the freedom to appear can never fully or adequately represent the people, since there are people who, we know, are missing from the public, missing from this public assembled here in Gezi Park; they are those who must find representation, even as those who seek to represent them risk imprisonment for doing so. And it is not just that there are some people who happen to be missing from the gathering because they had something else to do; rather, there are those who could not have gathered in Gezi Park, or can no longer gather, or who are indefinitely restrained from gathering. That very power of confinement is a way of defining, producing, and controlling what will be the public sphere and who will be admitted to public assembly. It works alongside privatization as a process that seeks to make public space into the entrepreneurial field of the market-driven state. So though we may wonder why it is that crowds that

gather to oppose privatization are broken up and dispersed by police force, gassing and physical assault, we have to remember that
the state that is off-loading public space to private enterprise, or
that now makes such decisions according to market values, is involved in at least two ways of controlling and decimating public
space. Some lament that a movement that begins by opposing
privatization inevitably becomes a movement that opposes police
violence. But let us try to see that the seizure of public space from
popular sovereignty is precisely the aim of both privatization and
police assaults on freedom of assembly. In this way as well, the
market and the prison work together in a prison industry that, as
Angela Davis has clearly shown, works to regulate rights of citizenship—and in the United States this happens in irrefutably racist
ways as black men continue to constitute the vast majority of prisoners.[11] We can add that the market and the prison work together
as well to constrict, decimate, and appropriate public space, se-
verely qualifying Hannah Arendt's notion of "the right to appear."

That said, I want to return to the theoretical point about freedom
of assembly in order to suggest some of the political implications
of how we think. My inquiry began with the following questions:
In what sense is freedom of assembly a punctual expression of
popular sovereignty? And does it have to be understood as a performative exercise, or what Jason Frank calls "the small dramas of
self-authorization"?[12] I began by suggesting that the performative
power of the people does not first rely on words. Assembly only
makes sense if bodies can and do gather or connect in some way,
and then speech acts that unfold from there articulate something
that is already happening at the level of the plural body. But let us
remember that vocalization is also a bodily act, as is sign language,
and this means that there is no speaking without the body signi-

fying something, and sometimes the body signifies something quite different from what a person actually says.

IN DEMOCRATIC THEORY, "we the people" is nevertheless first and foremost a speech act. Someone says "we" along with someone else, or some group says it together, perhaps chanting, or they write it and send it out into the world, or they stand one by one, or perhaps provisionally together, motionless and wordless, enacting assembly; when they say it, they seek to constitute themselves as "the people" from the moment in which it is declared. So considered as a speech act, "we the people" is an enunciation that seeks to bring about the social plurality it names. It does not describe that plurality, but gathers that group together through the speech act.

It would seem, then, that a linguistic form of autogenesis is at work in the expression "we the people"; it seems to be a rather magical act or, at least, one that compels us to believe in the magical nature of the performative. Of course, "we the people" starts a longer declaration of wants and desires, intended acts, and political claims. It is a preamble; it prepares the way for a specific set of assertions. It is a phrase that gets us ready for a substantive political claim, and yet, we have to pause at this way of starting up the sentence and ask whether a political claim is already being made, or is in the making even before someone speaks or signs. It is perhaps impossible for all the people who might say "we the people" at the same time to speak that phrase in unison. And if somehow an assembled group were to yell out, "we the people," as sometimes happens in the assemblies of the Occupy Movement, it is a brief and transitory moment, one in which a single person speaks at the same time that others speak, and some unintended plural sounding results from that concerted plural action, that speech act spoken in common, in sequence, with all the variations that repetition implies.

But let us admit that such a moment of literally speaking in unison, and naming ourselves as "the people," rarely happens quite like that—simultaneous and plural. After all, the declaration of "we the people" in the United States is a citation, and the phrase is never fully freed of its citationality. The Declaration of Independence of the United States begins with such a phrase, one that authorizes the writers to speak for the people more generally. It is a phrase that establishes political authority at the same time that it declares a form of popular sovereignty bound by no one political authority. Derrida has analyzed this in some very important ways, as has Bonnie Honig. Popular sovereignty can give itself (in assent) and withdraw itself (in dissent or in revolution), which means that every regime is dependent on it being given if it hopes to base its legitimacy on something other than coercion.

The speech act, however punctual, is nevertheless inserted in a citational chain, and that means that the temporal conditions for making the speech act precede and exceed the momentary occasion of its enunciation. And for yet another reason the speech act, however illocutionary, is not fully tethered to the moment of its enunciation: the social plurality designated and produced by the utterance cannot all assemble in the same place to speak at the same time, so it is both a spatially and temporally extended phenomenon. When and where popular sovereignty—the self-legislative power of the people—is "declared" or, rather, "declares itself," it is not exactly at a single instance, but instead in a series of speech acts or what I would suggest are *performative enactments* that are not restrictively verbal.

So I suppose my question might be formulated this way: What are the bodily conditions for the enunciation of "we the people," and do we make a mistake if we separate the matter of what we are free to say from how we are free to assemble? I propose to think about the assembly of bodies as a performative enactment, and so to suggest not only that (a) popular sovereignty is a performative exercise, but (b) it necessarily involves a performative enactment of bodies, sometimes assembled in the same place and sometimes not. First, I propose that we have to understand the idea of popular sovereignty that "we the people" seeks to secure.

If "we the people" set forth in the Constitution "declare a set of truths to be self-evident" as they apparently do in the Declaration of Independence, then we are already in a bit of a bind. A performative declaration seeks to bring about those truths, but if they are "self-evident" then they are precisely the kind of truths that don't need to be brought about at all. Either they are performatively induced or they are self-evident, but to bring about that which is self-evident seems paradoxical. We could say that a set of truths is being brought into being or we could say that we found those truths somewhere and that we did not bring them into being. Or we can say that the kind of truths at issue here have to be declared as self-evident for that self-evidence to be known. In other words, they have to be made evident, which means that they are not self-evident. This circularity seems to risk contradiction or tautology, but perhaps these truths only become evident in the manner in which they are declared. In other words, the performative enactment of the truth is the way of making evident that very truth, since the truth in question is not pregiven or static but enacted or exercised through a particular kind of plural action. If it is the very capacity for plural action that is at stake in claiming popular sovereignty, then there is no way to "show" this truth outside of the plural and invariably conflictual enactment we call self-constitution.

If the plural subject is constituted in the course of its performative action, then it is not already constituted; whatever form it has prior to its performative exercise is not the same as the form it takes as it acts, and after it has acted. So how do we then understand this movement of gathering, which is durational, and implies occasional, periodic, or definitive forms of scattering? It is not one act, but a convergence of actions different from one another, a form of political sociality irreducible to conformity. Even when a crowd speaks together, they have to gather in close enough proximity to hear each other's voice, to pace each person's own vocalization, to achieve rhythm and harmony to a sufficient degree, and so to achieve a relation both auditory and corporeal with those with whom some signifying action or speech act is undertaken. We start to speak *now* and stop *now*. We start to move *now,* or more or less at a given time, but certainly not as a single organism. We try to stop all at once, but some keep moving, and others move and rest at their own pace. Temporal seriality and coordination, bodily proximity, auditory range, coordinated vocalization—all of these constitute essential dimensions of assembly and demonstration. And they are all presupposed by the speech act that enunciates "we the people"; they are the complex elements of the *occasion* of that enunciation, the nonverbal forms of its signification.

If we try to take vocalization as the model of the speech act, then the body is surely presupposed as the organ of speech, both the organic condition and the vehicle of speech. The body is not transmuted into pure thought as it speaks, but signifies the organic conditions for verbalization, which means, according to Shoshana Felman, that the speech act is always doing something more and other than what it is actually saying. So just as there is no purely linguistic speech act separated from bodily acts, there is no purely conceptual moment of thought that does away with its own organic condition. And this tells us something about what it means to say "we the people," since whether it is written in a text or uttered on the street, it designates an assembly in the act of designating and forming itself. It acts on itself as it acts, and a corporeal condition of plurality is indexed whether or not it appears on the occasion of the utterance. That bodily condition, plural and dynamic, is a constitutive dimension of that occasion.

The embodied character of the people proves quite important to the kinds of demands that are made, since it is more often than not that basic bodily needs are not being met by virtue of the devastated ways of life. It may offend us theoretically to speak of "basic bodily needs," as if a certain ahistorical notion of the body is invoked for the purposes of making moral and political claims to fair treatment and the just distribution of public goods. But perhaps it would be even less acceptable to refuse to speak about bodily needs at all for fear of falling into a theoretical impasse. It is not a matter of accepting the ahistorical or historical version of the body, for even the formulation of historical construction has its invariant features, and every universal concept of the body is drawn from very specific historical formations. So neither side of that debate knows what kind of relation it is in to the other. Every particular bodily need can be articulated historically in one way or another, and it may well be that what is called a "need" is precisely a historical articulation of urgency that is not for that reason a mere effect of the articulation. In other words, there is no way to separate the idea of a bodily need from the representational scheme that differentially recognizes bodily needs and, too often, fails to recognize them at all. This does not make bodily needs fully ahistorical, but neither does it make them into pure effects of a specifically historical discourse. Once again, the relation between the body and discourse is chiastic, suggesting that the body has to be represented and that it is never fully exhausted by that representation. Moreover, the differential ways that it is and is not represented saturate the representation of needs in fields of power. One can also take into account the production of needs discussed by Marx and amplified theoretically by Agnes Heller[13] without claiming that "there is no such thing as a need." We could doubtless use other words, and trace the productive character of the words we use to amplify the phenomena, but we would still be talking about something, even if there is no way to get at that something without the language we use, even if we invariably transfigure that something by using the language we do. The notion of "needs" then would be an always already linguistically transfigured sense of requirement or urgency, and would be adequately captured neither by those synonyms nor by any others.

Similarly, the reference to the "organic" is both obligatory and vexed: the purely organic is no more recoverable than the purely conceptual, understood as nonorganic. Both notions appear as always organized in some way, belonging not to this or that discrete metaphysical substance, but to a cluster of relations, gestures, and movements that constitute the social sense of "organic" and very often regulate its metaphysical renditions. So, then, what other kinds of bodily actions and inactions, gestures, movements, and modes of coordination and organization condition and constitute the speech act, no longer understood restrictively as vocalization?

Sounds are but one way to signify in common—singing, chanting, declaring, beating drums or pots, or pounding against a prison or separation wall. How do all these kinds of acts "speak" in ways that index another sense of the organic and the political, one that might be understood as the performative enactment of assembly itself?

WHEN THOSE WHO FACE ACCELERATING prospects of precarity take to the streets and begin their claim with "we the people," then they are asserting that they, those who appear and speak there, are identified as "the people." They are working to ward off the prospect of oblivion. The phrase does not imply that those who profit are not "the people," and it does not necessarily imply a simple sense of inclusion: "we are the people, too." It can mean, "we are *still* the people"—therefore, still persisting and not yet destroyed. Or it can assert a form of equality in the face of increasing inequality; participants do this not simply by uttering that phrase, but by embodying equality to whatever extent that proves possible, constituting an assembly of the people on the grounds of equality. One might say, equality is experimentally and provisionally asserted in the midst of inequality, to which critics respond: this is vain and useless, since their acts are only symbolic, and true economic equality continues to become more elusive for those whose debts are astronomical and employment prospects foreclosed. And yet, it seems that the embodiment of equality in the practices of assembly, the insistence on interdependency and a fair distribution of labor tasks, the notion of a commonly held ground or "the commons," all start to put into the world a version of equality that is rapidly vanishing in other quarters. The point is not to regard the body merely as an instrument for making a political claim, but to let this body, the plurality of bodies, become the precondition of all further political claims.

Indeed, in the politics of the street that has been with us in the last years, in the Occupy Movement, Tahrir Square in its early stages, Puerta del Sol, Gezi Park, and the favela movement in Brazil, the basic requirements of the body are at the center of political mobilizations—*those requirements are, in fact, publicly enacted prior to any set of political demands.* Over and against forces of privatization, the destruction of public services and the ideals of the public good precipitated by the takeover of neoliberal forms of rationality in governance and everyday life, bodies require food and shelter, protection from injury and violence, and the freedom to move, to work, to have access to health care; bodies require other bodies for support and for survival.[14] It matters, of course, what age those bodies are, and whether they are able-bodied, since in all forms of dependency, bodies require not just one other person, but social systems of support that are complexly human and technical.

It is precisely in a world in which the supports for bodily life of increasing numbers of people are proving to be highly precarious that bodies are emerging together on the pavement or the dirt or along the wall that separates them from their land—this assembly, which can include virtual participants, still assumes a set of interlocking locations for a plural set of bodies. And in this way, the bodies belong to the pavement, the ground, the architecture, and the technology by which they live and move and work and desire. Although there are those who will say that active bodies assembled on the street constitute a powerful and surging multitude, one that in itself constitutes a radical democratic event or action, I can only partially agree with that view. When the people break off from established power, they enact the popular will, though to know that for certain, we would have to know who is breaking off, and where, and who does not break off, and where they are. There are, after all, all sorts of surging multitudes I would not want to endorse (even if I do not dispute their right to assemble), and they would include lynch mobs, anti-Semitic or racist or fascist congregations, and violent forms of antiparliamentary mass movements. I am less concerned with the ostensible vitality of surging multitudes or any nascent and promising life force that seems to belong to their collective action than I am with joining a struggle to establish more sustaining conditions of livability in the face of systematically induced precarity and forms of racial destitution. The final aim of politics is not simply to surge forth together (though this can be an essential moment of affective intensity within a broader struggle against precarity), constituting a new lived sense of the "people," even if sometimes, for the purposes of radical democratic change—which I do endorse—it is important to surge forth in ways that claim and alter the attention of the world for some more enduring possibility of livable life for all. It is one thing to feel alive, or to affirm aliveness, and yet another to say that that fleeting sense is all that we can expect from politics. Feeling alive is not quite the same as struggling for a world in which life becomes livable for those who have not yet been valued as living beings.

Although I understand that something has to hold such a group together, some demand, some felt sense of injustice and unlivability, some shared intimation of the possibility of change, there is also a desire to produce a new form of sociality on the spot. These mobilizations make their claims through language, action, gesture, and movement; through linking arms; through refusing to move;

through forming bodily modes of obstruction to police and state authorities. A given movement can move in and out of the space of heightened exposure, depending on its strategies and the military and police threats it must face. In each of these cases, however, we can say that these bodies form networks of resistance together, remembering that bodies who are active agents of resistance are also fundamentally in need of support. In resistance, vulnerability is not precisely converted into agency—it remains the condition of resistance, a condition of the life from which it emerges, the condition that, rendered as precarity, has to be opposed, and is opposed. This is something other than weakness or victimization, since, for the precarious, resistance requires exposing the abandoned or unsupported dimensions of life, but also mobilizing that vulnerability as a deliberate and active form of political resistance, an exposure of the body to power in the plural action of resistance.

IF THE BODY IN THE SPHERE of politics were by definition active—always self-constituting, never constituted—then we would not need to struggle for the conditions that allow the body its free activity in the name of social and economic justice. That struggle presumes that bodies are constrained and constrainable. The condition of bodily vulnerability is brought out into the open in those public assemblies and coalitions that seek to counter accelerating precarity. So it becomes all the more imperative to understand the relation between vulnerability and those forms of activity that mark our survival, our flourishing, as well as our political resistance. Indeed, even in the moment of actively appearing on the street, we are exposed, vulnerable to injury of one kind or another. This suggests that there are deliberate or willed mobilizations of vulnerability, what we might more aptly describe as political exposure.

Finally, let us remember that every claim we make to the public sphere is haunted by the prison, and anticipates the prison. In other words, in Gezi Park and on other streets in Turkey, to appear on the streets is to risk detention and imprisonment. And those medical professionals who came to help the protestors were arrested for trying to do so. And those lawyers who sought to defend those rights of assembly and expression were detained and arrested, and those human rights workers who sought to bring these crimes to the broader international public were also arrested or threatened with arrest. And those people in the media who sought to make known what had happened were also censored, detained, and arrested. Wherever the people sought to claim public space, they risked being stopped, injured, or imprisoned by the police. So when we think about public assembly, we are always thinking about the police power that either lets it happen or stops it from happening, and we are on guard against the moment in which the state starts to attack the people it is supposed to represent, at which point a forcible passage is established from public space to prison. Public space is effectively defined by that forcible passage. As a consequence, forms of solidarity with political prisoners—indeed, with all people incarcerated under unjust conditions—imply that solidarity must happen across the public sphere and the sphere of confinement. Prisoners are precisely those who are denied freedom of assembly and access to public space. So the very government movement to privatize state parks and to allow privatization to take the place of preserving public goods and public rights is a movement to establish police control over public space. There is no more effective way to do this than by imprisoning those who claim the right to public space, attacking and expelling protestors who seek to claim the public sphere for the public itself. That is one way to understand the arrest and detention of those who have fought the state as it wages its war on public life.

If privatization seeks to destroy public space, then prison is the ultimate way of barring access to public space. In this sense, then, privatization and prison work together to keep one out of the places where one knows that one belongs. No one can have the right to public assembly alone. As any of us claim that right, as we must, we have to do it with one another, in the midst of differences and disagreements, and in solidarity with those who have already lost that right or who have never been recognized as belonging to that public sphere. This is especially true for those who appear on the street without permits, who are opposing the police or the military or other security forces without weapons, who are transgendered in transphobic environments, who are undocumented in countries that criminalize those who seek rights of citizenship. To be short of protection is not a matter of becoming "bare life" but rather a concrete form of political exposure and potential struggle, at once concretely vulnerable, even breakable, and potentially and actively defiant, even revolutionary.

The bodies that assemble together designate and form themselves as "we the people," target those forms of abstraction that would act as if those social and bodily requirements for life can be destroyed as the result of neoliberal metrics and market rationalities that now act in the name of the public good. To show up in an assembly opposed to such destitution is precisely to enact the bodies for which we make such demands, which sometimes means making demands in another way than we intend. We do not have to know each other or deliberate in advance to make this demand for one another, since no body is really possible without those other bodies, linked, we might say, by the arm or in the name of another concept of democracy that demands new forms of solidarity on and off the street.

My strong view is that assemblies of this kind can succeed only if they subscribe to principles of nonviolence. There is an important place for principled embodied acts of nonviolence in the encounter with violence, and those acts must define any movement seeking to defend the rights of public assembly. Such a claim commits me to explaining how a principle is embodied, and I will try to indicate what I mean by that, but it also commits me to showing how the nonviolent resistance to violence is possible (an inquiry I will take up more fully in another context). The point about nonviolence that I wish to underscore is that it is not only a matter of holding a principle in mind, but letting a principle fashion one's comportment, even one's desire—one might say it is a matter of ceding to the principle. Nonviolent action is not simply a question of exercising the will to restrain oneself from acting out one's aggressive impulses; it is an active struggle with a cultivated form of constraint that takes corporeal and collective form.

Nonviolent resistance requires a body that appears, that acts, and that in its action seeks to constitute a different world from the one it encounters, and that means encountering violence without reproducing its terms. It does not just say no to a violent world, but crafts the self and its relation to the world in a new way, seeking to embody, however provisionally, the alternative for which it struggles. Can we then say that nonviolent resistance is performative? And is nonviolence an act, an ongoing activity, and, if so, what is its relation to passivity? Although passive resistance is one form of nonviolent action, not all forms of nonviolent action can be reduced to passive resistance.[15] The idea of lying flat before a tank, of "going limp" in the face of police power, involves a cultivated capacity to hold a certain position. The limp body may seem to have given up its agency, and yet, in becoming weight and obstruction, it persists in its pose. Aggression is not eradicated, but cultivated, and its cultivated form can be seen in the body as it stands, falls, gathers, stops, remains silent, takes on the support of other bodies that it itself supports. Supported and supporting, a certain notion of bodily interdependency is enacted that shows that nonviolent resistance should not be reduced to heroic individualism. Even the individual who moves out in front does so, in part, because she is backed by others.

Can we say that these are public acts of self-constitution, where the self is not just this or that individual self, but a social distribution of animated and interdependent selfhood with powers and freedom of expression, movement, and assembly, invoking and crafting bodies who manifest their basic entitlements to work, shelter, and sustenance?

Many difficulties stand in the way of realizing such an ideal. From the start, it is not always possible to define nonviolence with certainty. Indeed, every definition of nonviolence is an interpretation of what nonviolence is, or should be. This produces quandaries time and again: a principled view on nonviolence can sometimes be interpreted as violence, and when that happens, those who make the interpretation consider it to be the right one, and those whose action is being interpreted as violent consider it to be very wrong. When nonviolence is interpreted as violence, it is generally construed as a cover for violent aims or impulses, and so a ruse, or as a form of nonengagement that effectively allows those with force to prevail. It may be that one believes one is engaging in nonviolence only to realize that the action has some violent features or consequences, or that it enters into a gray zone, especially when force is used in the service of self-defense. But such unknowingness about the full implications of one's actions must be distinguished from active ways of distorting the action by those who seek to rename nonviolence as violence.

One might well consider tactics like strikes, hunger strikes in prison, work stoppages, nonviolent forms of occupying government or official buildings or spaces whose private status is being contested, or boycotts of various kinds, including consumer and cultural boycotts, sanctions, but also public assemblies, petitions, ways of refusing to recognize illegitimate authority, or declining to vacate institutions that have illegitimately been closed. What tends to unify such actions—or inactions, depending on your interpretation—is that they all call into question the legitimacy of a set of policies or actions, or the legitimacy of a specific form of rule. And yet, all of them can, by virtue of calling for a change in police, state formation, or rule, be called "destructive" since they do ask for a substantial alteration of the status quo. But if the repeal of a policy or a demand to form a state on a legitimate basis—both of which are clear exercises of the popular will under democracy—are deemed violent or, indeed, "terrorist," then a fatal confusion thwarts our ability to name nonviolent action in the context of democratic struggles.

In Gandhi's terms, drawing upon Thoreau, nonviolent civil disobedience is a "a civil breach of unmoral statutory enactments."[16] In his view, a law or statute can be regarded as unmoral, morally wrong, and so become the legitimate object of a civil action. So the statute is disobeyed, but because the statute is unmoral (or immoral), disobedience is right. It is a civil right to disobey an immoral public statute or law, since the realm of law is responsible to those forms of morality that Gandhi understands to structure civil life. We can certainly question whether morality underpins civil rights in the way that Gandhi assumes, but his general point seems important to accept. There are ways of questioning legitimacy that sometimes take the explicit form of speech acts; other times they rely on the expressive dimension of plural and embodied action or the refusal to act. When they do rely on plural and embodied action, they require embodied agency, and sometimes, when the police or security guards or the military try to break up and disperse a nonviolent assembly, that assembly comes into direct contact with other bodies, bodies that perhaps are wielding objects or guns that do physical harm. The risk of physical coercion and harm is assumed by those who engage in hunger strikes, since, for instance, the prisoner who refuses food not only refuses to obey an obligatory regulation, but fails to reproduce him- or herself as a prisoner. Indeed, the prison requires the physical reproduction of the prisoner in order to exercise its particular modality of force. In other words, nonviolent action sometimes takes place within a force field of violence, which is why nonviolence is rarely a position of purity and aloofness, that is, a position taken at a disengaged distance from the scene of violence. On the contrary, nonviolence happens within the scene of violence. Someone amiably and peaceably walking down the street is neither engaging in violence nor practicing nonviolence. Nonviolence comes into play with the threat of violence: it is a way of holding and comporting oneself on one's own and with others in a potentially or actually conflictual space. That is not to say that nonviolence is only reactive: it can be a way of approaching a situation, even living in the world, a daily practice of mindfulness that attends to the precarious character of living beings.

Precisely because nonviolence is a deliberate way of holding an embodied self in the face of conflict, or in the middle of conflictual urges and provocations, it has to call upon a practice of nonviolence that precedes and anticipates the moment of decision itself. This form of holding oneself, this posture of reflexivity, is mediated through historical conventions that serve as the recognizable basis for nonviolent action. Even if nonviolence seems like a solitary act, it is mediated socially, and it depends upon the persistence and recognition of conventions governing nonviolent modes of conduct.

Of course, there are those who break off and decide on violent methods, or those who enter nonviolent assemblies seeking to divert its purposes, and they must also be resisted. Violence is a constitutive possibility of every assembly, not just because the police are usually waiting in the wings, and not just because there are violent factions seeking to appropriate nonviolent assemblies, but because no political assembly can ever fully overcome its own constitutive antagonisms. The task is to find a way to cultivate antagonism into a nonviolent practice. But the idea that we might find and inhabit some peaceful region of political subjectivity underestimates the pressing and continuous task of articulating aggression and antagonism into the substance of democratic contest. There is no way to achieve nonviolence without the tactical and principled cultivation of aggression into embodied modes of action. We can mime the gestures of violence as a way of signifying not what we aim to do, but the rage we feel and the rage we limit and transfigure into embodied political expression. There are many ways to get physical without doing harm, and those are the ways we surely should pursue.

In the end, it is probably not possible to think about tactics of nonviolence outside of their particular historical contexts. It is not an absolute rule, but perhaps more precisely defined as an ethos; indeed, every tactic has its implicit ethos. For nonviolence is both *ethos* and *tactic,* and that means that nonviolent movements, such as boycotts and strikes, cannot simply be war by other means. They have to show themselves to be substantial ethical alternatives to war, for it is only through the manifestation of the ethical claim that the political value of the position can be seen. Such a demonstration is not easy to do when there are those who can only read the tactic as hatred and the continuation of war by other means. This is doubtless one reason that nonviolence is established not only by what we do, but by how it appears, which means that we require the media that can let nonviolence be recognized as such.

Chapter 6

Can One Lead a Good Life in a Bad Life?

I would like to follow up on a question that Adorno posed, one that is still alive for us today. It is a question to which I return time and again, one that continues to make itself felt in a recurrent way. There is no easy way to answer the question, and certainly no easy way to escape its claim upon us. Adorno, of course, told us in *Minima Moralia* that "Es gibt kein richtiges Leben im falschen" ("Wrong life cannot be lived rightly," in Jephcott's translation),[1] and yet, this did not lead him to despair of the possibility of morality. Indeed, we are left with the question, how does one lead a good life in a bad life? He underscored the difficulty of finding a way to pursue a good life for oneself, as oneself, in the context of a broader world that is structured by inequality, exploitation, and forms of effacement. That would at least be the initial way I would reformulate his question. Indeed, as I reformulate it for you now, I am aware that it is a question that takes new form depending on the historical time in which it is formulated. So, from the beginning, we have two problems: The first is how to live one's own life well, such that we might say that we are living a good life within a world in which the good life is structurally or systematically foreclosed for so many, or becomes a phrase that makes no sense, or seems to denote a way of life that is in some ways quite bad. The second problem is, what form does this question take for us now? Or how does the historical time in which we live condition and permeate the form of the question itself?

Before I go further, I am compelled to reflect on the terms we use. Indeed, "the good life" is a controversial phrase, since there are so many different views on what "the good life" (*das Richtige Leben*) might be. Many have identified the good life with economic well-being, prosperity, or even security, but we know that both economic well-being and security can be achieved by those who are not living a good life. And this is most clear when those who claim to live the good life do so by profiting off the labor of others, or relying on an economic system that entrenches forms of inequality. So "the good life" has to be defined more broadly so that it does not presuppose or imply inequality, or it has to be reconciled with other normative values. If we rely on ordinary language to tell us what the good life is, we will become confused, since the phrase has become a vector for competing schemes of value.

In fact, we might conclude rather quickly that, on the one hand, "the good life" as a phrase belongs either to an outdated Aristotelian formulation, tied to individualistic forms of moral conduct, or, on the other hand, that "the good life" has been too contaminated by commercial discourse to be useful to those who want to think about the relationship between morality, or ethics more broadly, and social and economic theory. When Adorno queries whether it is possible to lead a good life in a bad life, he is asking about the relation of moral conduct to social conditions, but more broadly about the relation of morality to social theory; indeed, he is also asking how the broader operations of power and domination enter into, or disrupt, our individual reflections on how best to live. He writes, "das ethische Verhalten oder das moralische oder unmoralische Verhalten immer ein gesellschaftliches Phänomen ist—das heist, da es überhaupt keinen Sinn hat, vom ethischen und vom moralischen Verhalten unter Absehung der Beziehungen der Menschen zueinander zu reden, und da das rein für sich selbst seiende Individuum eine ganz leere Abstraktion ist" ["ethical conduct or moral and immoral conduct is always a social phenomenon— in other words, it makes absolutely no sense to talk about ethical and moral conduct separately from relations of human beings to each other, and an individual who exists purely for himself is an empty abstraction"].[2] Or again, "die gesellschaftlichen Kategorien bis ins Innerste der moralphilosophie sich hinein erstrecken" ["social categories enter into the very fiber of those of moral philosophy"].[3] Or yet again, in his final sentence of *Probleme der Moralphilosophie*: "Kurz, also was Moral heute vielleicht überhaupt noch heissen darf, das geht über an die Frage nach der Einrichtung der Welt—man könnte sagen: die Frage nach dem richtigen Leben wäre die Frage nach der richtigen Politik selber heute im Bereich des zu Verwirklichenden gelegen wäre" ["anything that we can call morality today merges into the question of the organization of the world . . . we might even say that the quest for the good life is the quest for the right form of politics, if indeed such a right form of politics lay within the realm of what can be achieved today"].[4] And so it makes sense to ask, which social configuration of "life" enters into the question, how best to live? If I ask how best to live, or how to lead a good life, I seem not only to draw upon ideas of what is good, but also what is living, and what is life. I must have a sense of my life in order to ask what kind of life to lead, and my life must appear to me as something I might lead, something that does not just lead me. And yet, it is clear that I cannot "lead" all aspects of the living organism that I am, even though I am compelled to ask, how might I lead my life? How does one lead a life when not all life processes that make up a life can be led, or when only certain aspects of a life can be directed or formed in a deliberate or reflective way, and others clearly not?

So if the question, how am I to lead a good life? is one of the elementary questions of morality, indeed perhaps its defining question, then it would seem that morality from its inception is bound up with biopolitics. By biopolitics, I mean those powers that organize life, even the powers that differentially dispose lives to precarity as part of a broader management of populations through governmental and nongovernmental means, and that establish a set of measures for the differential valuation of life itself. In asking how to lead my life, I am already negotiating such forms of power. The most individual question of morality—how do I live this life that is mine?—is bound up with biopolitical questions distilled in forms such these: Whose lives matter? Whose lives do not matter as lives, are not recognizable as living, or count only ambiguously as alive? Such questions presume that we cannot take for granted that all living humans bear the status of a subject who is worthy of rights and protections, with freedom and a sense of political belonging; on the contrary, such a status must be secured through political means, and where it is denied, that deprivation must be made manifest. It has been my suggestion that to understand the differential way that that such a status is allocated, we must ask whose lives are grievable, and whose are not? The biopolitical management of the ungrievable proves crucial to approaching the question, how do I lead this life? And how do I live this life within the life, the conditions of living, that structure us now? At stake is the following sort of inquiry: Whose lives are already considered not lives, or only partially living, or already dead and gone, prior to any explicit destruction or abandonment?

Of course, this question becomes most acute for someone, anyone, who already understands him- or herself to be a dispensable sort of being, one who registers at an affective and corporeal level that his or her life is *not* worth safeguarding, protecting, and valuing. This is someone who understands that she or he will *not* be grieved if his or her life is lost, and so one for whom the conditional claim "I would not be grieved" is actively lived in the present moment. If it turns out that I have no certainty that I will have food or shelter, or that no social network or institution would catch me if I fall, then I come to belong to the ungrievable. This does not mean that there won't be some who grieve me, or that the ungrievable do not have ways of grieving one another. It doesn't mean that I won't be grieved in one corner and not in another, or that the loss doesn't register at all. But these forms of persistence and resistance still take place within the shadow-life of the public, occasionally breaking out and contesting those schemes by which they are devalued by asserting their collective value. So, yes, the ungrievable gather sometimes in public insurgencies of grief, which is why in so many countries it is difficult to distinguish the funeral from the demonstration.

So I overstate the case, but I do it for a reason. The reason that someone will not be grieved, or has already been established as one who is not to be grieved, is that there is no present structure of support that will sustain that life, which implies that it is devalued, not worth supporting and protecting as a life by dominant schemes of value. The very future of my life depends upon that condition of support, so if I am not supported, then my life is established as tenuous, precarious, and in that sense not worthy to be protected from injury or loss, and so not grievable. If only a grievable life can be valued, and valued through time, then only a grievable life will be eligible for social and economic support, housing, health care, employment, rights of political expression, forms of social recognition, and conditions for political agency. One must, as it were, be grievable before one is lost, before any question of being neglected or abandoned, and one must be able to live a life knowing that the loss of this life that I am would be mourned and so every measure will be taken to forestall this loss.

But if one is alive at the same time that one registers that the life one is living will never be considered losable or lost, precisely because it was never considered a life, or was already considered lost, then how do we understand this shadowy domain of existence, this modality of nonbeing in which populations nevertheless live? From within a felt sense that one's life is ungrievable or dispensable, how does the moral question get formulated, and how does the demand for public grieving take place? In other words, how do I endeavor to lead a good life if I do not have a life to speak of, or when the life that I seek to lead is considered dispensable, or is in fact already abandoned? When the life that I lead is unlivable, a rather searing paradox follows, for the question, how do I lead a good life? presumes that *there are lives* to be led, that is, that there are lives recognized as living and that mine is among them. Indeed, the question presumes as well that there is an *I* who has the power to pose the question reflexively, and that I also appear to myself, which means that I can appear within the field of appearance that is available to me. For the question to be viable, the one who asks it must be able to pursue whatever answer emerges. For the question to clear a path that *I* can follow, the world must be structured in such a way that my reflection and action prove not only possible but efficacious. If I am to deliberate on how best to live, then I have to presume that the life I seek to pursue can be affirmed as a life, that I can affirm it, even if it is not affirmed more generally, or even under those conditions when it is not always easy to discern whether there is a social and economic affirmation of my life. After all, this life that is mine is reflected back to me from a world that is disposed to allocate the value of life differentially, a world in which my own life is valued more or less than others. In other words, this life that is mine reflects back to me a problem of equality and power and, more broadly, the justice or injustice of the allocation of value.

So if this sort of world, what we might be compelled to call "the bad life," fails to reflect back my value as a living being, then I must become critical of those categories and structures that produce that form of effacement and inequality. In other words, I cannot affirm my own life without critically evaluating those structures that differentially value life itself. This practice of critique is one in which my own life is bound up with the objects that I think about. My life is this life, lived here, in the spatiotemporal horizon established by my body, but it is also out there, implicated in other living processes of which I am but one. Further, it is implicated in the power differentials that decide whose life matters more, and whose life matters less, whose life becomes a paradigm for all living things, and whose life becomes a nonlife within the contemporary terms that govern the value of living beings. Adorno remarks that "Man muss an dem Normativen, an der Selbstkritik, an der Frage nach dem Richtigen oder Falschen

und gleichzeitig an der Kritik der Fehlbarkeit der Instanz fest-
halten, die eine solche Art der Selbstkritik sich zutraut" ["we need
to hold fast to moral norms, to self-criticism, to the question of
right and wrong, and at the same time to a sense of the fallibility
of the authority that has the confidence to undertake such self-
criticism"].[5] This "I" may not be as knowing about itself as it claims,
and it may well be true that the only terms by which this I grasps
itself are those that belong to a discourse that precedes and informs
thought without any of us being able fully to grasp its working
and its effect. And since values are defined and distributed through
modes of power whose authority must be questioned, I am in a
certain bind. Do I establish myself in the terms that would make
my life valuable, or do I offer a critique of the reigning order of
values?

So though I must and do ask, how shall I live a good life? and this
aspiration is an important one. I have to think carefully about this
life that is mine, that is also a broader social life, that is connected
with other living beings in ways that engage me in a critical relation to the discursive orders of life and value in which I live or,
rather, in which I endeavor to live. What gives them their authority? And is that authority legitimate? Since my own life is
at stake in such an inquiry, the critique of the biopolitical order is
a living issue for me, and as much as the potential for living a good
life is at stake, so too is the struggle to live and the struggle to live
within a just world. Whether or not I can live a life that has value
is not something that I can decide on my own, since it turns out
that this life is and is not my own, and that this is what makes me
a social creature, and a living one. The question of how to live the
good life, then, is already, and from the start, bound up with this
ambiguity, and it is bound up with a living practice of critique.

If I am not able to establish my value in the world in any more than a transient way, then my sense of possibility is equally transient. The moral imperative to lead a good life, and the reflective questions it engenders, can both sometimes seem very cruel and unthinking to those who live in conditions of hopelessness; and we can perhaps easily understand the cynicism that sometimes envelops the very practice of morality: Why should I act morally, or even ask the question of how best to live, if my life is already not considered to be a life, if my life is already treated as a form of death, or if I belong to what Orlando Patterson has called the realm of "social death"—a term he used to describe the condition of living under slavery?[6]

Because contemporary forms of economic abandonment and dispossession that follow from the institutionalization of neoliberal rationalities or the differential production of precarity cannot for the most part be analogized with slavery, it remains important to distinguish among modalities of social death. Perhaps we cannot use one word to describe the conditions under which lives becomes unlivable, yet the term "precarity" can distinguish between modes of "unlivability": those who, for instance, belong to imprisonment without recourse to due process; those who characterize living in war zones or under occupation, exposed to violence and destruction without recourse to safety or exit; those who undergo forced emigration and live in liminal zones, waiting for borders to open, food to arrive, and the prospect of living with documentation; those who mark the condition of being part of a dispensable or expendable workforce for whom the prospect of a stable livelihood seems increasingly remote, and who live in a daily way within a collapsed temporal horizon, suffering a sense of a damaged future in the stomach and in the bones, trying to feel but fearing more what might be felt. How can one ask how best to lead a life when one feels no power to direct life, when one is uncertain that one is alive, or when one is struggling to feel the sense that one is alive, but also fearing that feeling, and the pain of living in this way? Under contemporary conditions of forced emigration and neoliberalism, vast populations now live with no sense of a secure future, no sense of continuing political belonging, living a sense of damaged life as part of the daily experience of neoliberalism.

I do not mean to say that the struggle for survival precedes the domain of morality or moral obligation as such, since we know that even under conditions of extreme threat, people do offer whatever acts of support are possible. We know this from some of the extraordinary reports from the concentration camps. In the work of Robert Antelme, for instance, it could be the exchange of a cigarette between those who share no common language, but find themselves in the same condition of imprisonment and peril in the concentration camp. Or in the work of Primo Levi, the response to the other can take the form of simply listening to, and recording, the details of the story that the other might tell, letting that story become part of an undeniable archive, the enduring trace of loss that compels the ongoing obligation to mourn; or in the work of Charlotte Delbo, the sudden offering to another of the last piece of bread that one desperately needs for oneself. And yet, in these same accounts, there are also those who will not extend the hand, who will take the bread for oneself, hoard the cigarette, and sometimes suffer the anguish of depriving another under conditions of radical destitution. In other words, under conditions of extreme peril and heightened precarity, the moral dilemma does not pass away; it persists precisely in the tension between wanting to live and wanting to live in a certain way with others. One is still in small and vital ways "leading a life" as one recites or hears the story, as one affirms whatever occasion there might be to acknowledge the life and suffering of another. Even the utterance of a name can come as the most extraordinary form of recognition, especially when one has become nameless or when one's name has been replaced by a number, or when one is not addressed at all.

At a controversial moment, in speaking about the Jewish people, Hannah Arendt made clear that it was not enough for the Jews to struggle for survival, and that survival cannot be the end or goal of life itself.[7] Citing Socrates, she insisted on the crucial distinction between the desire to live and the desire to live well or, rather, the desire to live the good life.[8] For Arendt, survival was not, and should not be, a goal in itself, since life itself was not an intrinsic good. Only the good life makes life worth living. She resolved that Socratic dilemma quite easily but perhaps too quickly, or so it seems to me. I am not sure her answer can work for us, nor am I convinced that it ever did quite work. For Arendt, the life of the body had for the most part to be separated from the life of the mind, which is why in *The Human Condition* she drew a distinction between the public and private spheres. The private sphere included the domain of need, the reproduction of material life, sexuality, life, death, and transience. She clearly understood that the private sphere supported the public sphere of action and thought, but in her view, the political is defined by action, including the active sense of speaking. So the verbal deed became the action of the deliberative and public space of politics. Those who entered into the public sphere did so from the private sphere, so the public sphere depended fundamentally on the reproduction of the private and the clear passageway that led from the private to the public. Those who could not speak Greek, who came from else-where and whose speech was not intelligible, were considered barbarians, which means that the public sphere was not conceived as a space of multilingualism and so failed to imply the practice of translation as a public obligation. And yet, we can see that the ef-ficacious verbal act depended on (a) a stable and sequestered pri-vate sphere that reproduced the masculine speaker and actor and (b) a language designated for verbal action, the defining feature of politics, that could be heard and understood because it conformed to the demands of monolingualism. The public sphere, defined by an intelligible and efficacious set of speech acts, was thus perpetu-ally shadowed by the problems of unrecognized labor (women and slaves) and multilingualism. And the site where both converge was precisely the situation of the slave, one who could be replaced, whose political status was null, and whose language was consid-ered no language at all.

Of course, Arendt understood that the body was important to any conception of action, and that even those who fight in resis-tances or in revolutions had to undertake bodily actions to claim their rights and to create something new.[9] And the body was certainly important to public speech, understood as a verbal form of action. The body appears again as a central figure in her impor-tant conception of natality, which is linked with her conception of both aesthetics and politics. After all, the kind of action under-stood as "giving birth" is not quite the same as the action involved in revolution, and yet both are bound together by the fact that they are different ways of creating something new, without precedent. If there is suffering in acts of political resistance or, indeed, in giving birth, it is a suffering that serves the purpose of bringing something new into the world. And yet, what do we make of that suffering that belongs to forms of labor that slowly or quickly destroy the body of the laborer, or other forms that serve no instrumental purpose at all? If we define politics restrictively as an active stance, verbal and physical, that takes place within a clearly demarcated public sphere, then it seems we are left to call "useless suffering" and unrecognized labor the prepolitical—experiences, not actions, that exist outside the political as such. However, since any conception of the political has to take into account what operation of power demarcates the political from the prepolitical, and how the distinction between public and private accords differential value to different life processes, we have to refuse the Arendtian definition, even as it gives us much to value. Or, rather, we have to take the Arendtian distinction between the life of the body and the life of the mind as a point of departure for thinking about a different kind of bodily politics. After all, Arendt does not simply distinguish mind and body in a Cartesian sense; rather, she affirms only those forms of embodied thought and action that create something new, that undertake action with performative efficacy.

Actions that are performative are irreducible to technical applications, and they are differentiated from passive and transient forms of experience. Thus, when and where there is suffering or transience, it is there to be transformed into the life of action and thought, and that action and thought has to be performative in the illocutionary sense, modeled on aesthetic judgment, bringing something new into the world. This means that the body concerned solely with the issues of survival, with the reproduction of material conditions and the satisfaction of basic needs, is not yet the "political" body; the private is necessary, to be sure, since the political body can only emerge into the light of public space to act and think if it is well fed and well sheltered, supported by numerous prepolitical actors whose action is not political. If there is no political actor who cannot assume that the private domain operates as support, then the political defined as the public is essentially dependent on the private, which means that the private is not the opposite of the political, but enters into its very definition. This well-fed body speaks openly and publicly; this body who spent the night sheltered and in the private company of others emerges always later to act in public. That private sphere becomes the very background of public action, but should it for that reason be cast as prepolitical? Does it, for instance, matter whether relations of equality or dignity or nonviolence exist in that shadowy background where women, children, the elderly, and slaves dwell? If one sphere of inequality is disavowed in order to justify and promote another sphere of equality, then surely we need a politics that can name and expose that very contradiction and the operation of disavowal by which it is sustained. If we accept the definition Arendt proposes between public and private, we run the risk of ratifying that disavowal.

So, what is at stake here in revisiting Arendt's account of the private and public distinction in the classical Greek polis? The disavowal of dependency becomes the precondition of the autonomous thinking and acting political subject, which immediately raises the question of what kind of "autonomous" thought and action this might be. And if we agree to the private and public distinction that Arendt presents, we accept that disavowal of dependency as a precondition of politics rather than taking those mechanisms of disavowal as the objects of our own critical analysis. Indeed, it is the critique of that unacknowledged dependency that establishes the point of departure for a new body politics, one that begins with an understanding of human dependency and interdependency, one that, in other words, can account for the relation between precarity and performativity.

Indeed, what if one started with the condition of dependency and the norms that facilitate its disavowal? What difference would such a point of departure make to the idea of politics, and even to the role of performativity within the political? Is it possible to separate the agentic and active dimension of performative speech from the other dimensions of bodily life, including dependency and vulnerability, modes of the living body that cannot easily or fully be transformed into forms of unambiguous action? We would not only need to let go of the idea that verbal speech distinguishes the human from nonhuman animals, but we would need to affirm those dimensions of speaking that do not always reflect conscious and deliberate intention. Indeed, sometimes, as Wittgenstein has remarked, we speak, we utter words, and only later have a sense of their life. My speech does not start with my intention, though something we surely can call intention certainly gets formed as we speak. Moreover, the performativity of the human animal takes place through gesture, gait, modes of mobility, sound and image, and various expressive means that are not reducible to public forms of verbal speech. That republican ideal is yet to give way to a broader understanding of sensate democracy. The way we gather on the street, sing or chant, or even maintain our silence can be, is, part of the performative dimension of politics, situating speech as one bodily act among others. So bodies act when they speak, to be sure, but speaking is not the only way that bodies act—and certainly not the only way they act politically. And when public demonstrations or political actions have as their aim the opposition to failing forms of support—lack of food or shelter, unreliable or uncompensated labor—then what was previously understood as the "background" of politics becomes its explicit object. When people gather to rally against induced conditions of precarity, they are acting performatively, giving embodied form to the Arendtian idea of concerted action. But at such moments, the performativity of politics emerges from conditions of precarity, and in political opposition to that precarity. When populations are abandoned by economic or political policy, then lives are deemed unworthy of support. Over and against such policies, the contemporary politics of performativity insists upon the interdependency of living creatures as well as the ethical and political obligations that follow from any policy that deprives, or seeks to deprive, a population of a livable life. The politics of perfomativity is also a way of enunciating and enacting value in the midst of a biopolitical scheme that threatens to devalue such populations.

Of course, this discussion brings us to another question: Are we speaking only about human bodies? We have mentioned that bodies cannot be understood at all without the environments, the machines, and the social organization of interdependency upon which they rely, all of which form the conditions of their persistence and flourishing. And finally, even if we come to understand and enumerate the requirements of the body, do we struggle only for those requirements to be met? As we have seen, Arendt surely opposed that view. Or do we struggle as well for bodies to thrive, and for lives to become livable? As I hope to have suggested, we cannot struggle for a good life, a livable life, without meeting the requirements that allow a body to persist. It is necessary to demand that bodies have what they need to survive, for survival is surely a precondition for all other claims we make. And yet, that demand proves insufficient since we survive precisely in order to live, and life, as much as it requires survival, must be *more* than survival in order to be livable. One can survive without being able to live one's life. And in some cases, it surely does not seem worth it to survive under such conditions. So, an overarching demand must be precisely for a livable life, that is, a life that can be lived.

How, then, do we think about a livable life without positing a single or uniform ideal for that life? As I indicated in earlier chapters, it is not a matter, in my view, of finding out what the human really is, or should be, since it has surely been made plain that humans are animals, too, and that their very bodily existence depends upon systems of support that are both human and nonhuman. So, to a certain extent, I follow my colleague Donna Haraway in asking us to think about the complex relationalities that constitute bodily life, and in suggesting that we do not need any more ideal forms of the human; rather, we need to understand and attend to the complex set of relations without which we do not exist at all.[10]

Of course, there are conditions under which the kind of dependency and relationality to which I am referring seems to be unbearable. If a laborer depends on an employer by whom he or she is exploited, then that laborer's dependency appears to be equivalent to his or her capacity to be exploited. One might resolve that one has to do away with all dependency since the social form that dependency assumes is exploitation. And yet it would be an error to identify the contingent form that dependency takes under conditions of exploitative labor relations with the final or necessary meaning of dependency. Even if dependency always takes one social form or another, it remains something that can and does transfer among those forms, and so proves to be irreducible to any one of them. Indeed, my stronger point is simply this: no human creature survives or persists without depending on a sustaining environment, social forms of relationality, and economic forms that presume and structure interdependency. It is true that dependency implies vulnerability, and sometimes that vulnerability is precisely to forms of power that threaten or diminish our existence. And yet, this does not mean that we can legislate against dependency or the condition of vulnerability to social forms. Indeed, we could not begin to understand why it is so difficult to live a good life in a bad life if we were invulnerable to those forms of power that exploit or manipulate our desire to live. We desire to live, even to live well, within social organizations of life, biopolitical regimes, that sometimes establish our very lives as disposable or negligible or, worse, seek to negate our lives. If we cannot persist without social forms of life, and if the only available ones are those that work against the prospect of our living, we are in a difficult bind, if not an impossible one.

Put in yet other words, we are, as bodies, vulnerable to others and to institutions, and this vulnerability constitutes one aspect of the social modality through which bodies persist. The issue of *my* or *your* vulnerability implicates us in a broader political problem of equality and inequality, since vulnerability can be projected and denied (psychological categories), but also exploited and manipulated (social and economic categories) in the course of producing and naturalizing forms of social inequality. This is what is meant by the unequal distribution of vulnerability.

My normative aim, however, is not simply to call for an equal distribution of vulnerability, since much depends on whether the social form of vulnerability that is being distributed is itself a livable one. In other words, one does not want everyone to have an equally unlivable life. As much as equality is a necessary goal, it remains insufficient if we do not know how best to evaluate whether or not the social form of vulnerability to be distributed is just. On the one hand, I am arguing that the disavowal of dependency and, in particular, the social form of vulnerability to which it gives rise, works to establish a distinction between those who are dependent and those who are not. And this distinction works in the service of inequality, shoring up forms of paternalism, or casting those in need in essentialist terms. On the other hand, I am suggesting that only through a concept of interdependency that affirms the bodily dependency, conditions of precarity, and potentials for performativity can we think a social and political world that seeks to overcome precarity in the name of livable lives.

In my view, vulnerability constitutes one aspect of the political modality of the body, where the body is surely human, but understood as a human animal. Vulnerability to one another, that is to say, even when conceived as reciprocal, marks a precontractual dimension of our social relations. This means as well that at some level it defies that instrumental logic that claims that I will only protect your vulnerability if you protect mine (wherein politics becomes a matter of brokering a deal or making a calculation on chances). In fact, vulnerability constitutes one of the conditions of sociality and political life that cannot be contractually stipulated, and whose denial and manipulability constitute an effort to destroy or manage an interdependent social condition of politics. As Jay Bernstein has made clear, vulnerability cannot be associated exclusively with injurability. All responsiveness to what happens is a function and effect of vulnerability, whether it is an openness to registering a history that has not yet been told, or a receptivity to what another body undergoes or has undergone, even when that body is gone. As I have suggested, bodies are always in some sense outside themselves, exploring or navigating their environment, extended and even sometimes dispossessed through the senses. If we can become lost in another, or if our tactile, motile, haptic, visual, olfactory, or auditory capacities comport us beyond ourselves, that is because the body does not stay in its own place, and because dispossession of this kind characterizes bodily sense more generally. When being dispossessed in sociality is regarded as a constitutive function of what it means to live and persist, what difference does that make to the idea of politics itself?

If we then return to our original question, how is it that I might lead a good life in a bad life? we can rethink this moral question in light of social and political conditions without thereby eradicating the moral importance of the question. It may be that the question of how to live a good life depends upon having the power to lead a life as well as the sense of having a life, living a life, or indeed, the sense of being alive.

There is always the possibility of a cynical response, according to which the point is precisely to forget morality and its individualism and dedicate oneself to the struggle for social justice. Pursuing this path, then, we might conclude that morality has to cede its place to politics in the broadest sense, that is, as a common project to realize ideals of justice and equality in ways that are universalizable. Of course, to arrive at this conclusion, there is still a nagging and obdurate problem, namely, that there is still this "I" who must in some way enter into, negotiate, and undertake a practice within a broader social and political movement; and when that movement seeks to displace or eradicate this "I" and the problem of its own "life," then another form of effacement happens, an absorption into a common norm, and so a destruction of the living I. It cannot be that the question of how best to live this life, or how to lead a good life, culminates in the effacement or destruction of this "I" and its "life." Or if it does, then the way the question is answered leads to the destruction of the question itself. And though I do not think that the question of morality can be posed outside of the context of social and economic life, without presupposing something about who counts as a subject of life, or as a living subject, I am quite sure that the answer to the question of how best to live cannot be rightly answered by destroying the subject of life.

And yet, if we return to Adorno's claim that it is not possible to live a good life in a bad life, we see that the term "life" occurs twice, and this is not simply incidental. If I ask how to lead a good life, then I am seeking recourse to a "life" that would be good whether or not I was the one who might be leading it, and yet I am the one who needs to know, and so in some sense it is my life. In other words, already, from within the perspective of morality, life itself is doubled. By the time I get to the second part of the sentence, and I seek to know how to live a good life in a bad life, I am confronted with an idea of life as socially and economically organized. That social and economic organization of life is "bad" precisely because it does not provide the conditions for a livable life, because the livability is unequally distributed. One might wish simply to live a good life in the midst of a bad life, finding one's own way as best as one can and disregarding the broader social and economic inequalities that are produced through specific organizations of life, but it is not so simple. After all, the life I am living, though clearly this life and not some other, is already connected with broader networks of life, and if it were not connected with such networks, I could not actually live. So my own life depends on a life that is not mine, not just the life of the other, but a broader social and economic organization of life. So my own living, my survival, depends on this broader sense of life, one that includes organic life, living and sustaining environments, and social networks that affirm and support interdependency. They constitute who I am, which means that I cede some part of my distinctively human life in order to live, in order to be human at all.

Implicit in the question of how to live a good life in a bad life is the idea that we might still think about what a good life might be, that we can no longer think of it exclusively in terms of the good life of the individual. If there are two such "lives"—my life and the good life, understood as a social form of life—then the life of the one is implicated in the life of the other. And this means that when we speak about social lives, we are referring to how the social traverses the individual, or even establishes the social form of individuality. At the same time, the individual, no matter how intensively self-referential, is always referring to itself through a mediating form, through some media, and its very language for recognizing itself comes from elsewhere. The social conditions and mediates this recognition of myself that I undertake. As we know from Hegel, the "I" who comes to recognize itself, its own life, recognizes itself always also as *another's* life. The reason why the "I" and the "you" are ambiguous is that they are each bound up in other systems of interdependency, what Hegel calls *Sittlichkeit*. And this means that although I perform that recognition of myself, some set of social norms is being worked out in the course of that performance that I author, and whatever is being worked out does not originate with me, even as I am not thinkable without it.

In Adorno's *Probleme der Moralphilosophie,* what begins as a moral question about how to pursue the good life in a bad life culminates in the claim that there must be resistance to the bad life in order to pursue the good life. This is what he writes: "das Leben selbst eben so entstellt und verzerrt ist, dass im Grunde kein Mensch in ihm richtig zu leben, seine eigene menschliche Bestimmung zu realisieren vermag—ja, ich möchte fast so weit gehen: dass die Welt so eingerichtet ist, dass selbst noch die einfachste Forderung von Integrität und Anständigkeit eigentlich fast bei einem jeden Menschen überhaupt notwendig zu Protest führen muss" ["life itself is so deformed and distorted that no one is able to live the good life in it or to fulfil his destiny as a human being. Indeed, I would almost go so far as to say that, given the way the world is organized, even the simplest demand for integrity and decency must necessarily lead almost everyone to protest"].[11] It is interesting that at such a moment Adorno would claim that he *almost* (*fast*) goes so far as to say what he then says. He is not sure the formulation is quite right, but he goes ahead anyway. He overrides his hesitation, but keeps it nevertheless on the page. Can it be so simply said that the pursuit of the moral life can and must, under contemporary conditions, culminate in protest? Can resistance be reduced to protest? Or, further, is protest for Adorno in the social form that the pursuit of the good life now takes? That same speculative character continues as he remarks that "Das einzige, was man vielleicht sagen kann, ist, dass das richtige Leben heute in der Gestalt des Widerstandes gegen die von dem fortgeschrittensten Bewusstsein durchschauten, kritisch aufgelösten Formen eines falschen Lebens bestünde" ["The only thing that can perhaps be said is that the good life today would consist in resistance to forms of the bad life that have been seen through and critically dissected by the most progressive minds"].[12] In the German, Adorno refers to a "false" life, and this is translated into

English as "the bad life"—of course, the difference is quite important, since for morality, the pursuit of the good life may well be a true life, but the relation between the two has yet to be explained. Further, it seems that Adorno appoints himself to the elect group of those who are progressive and capable enough to conduct the critical activity that must be pursued. Significantly, that practice of critique is rendered synonymous with "resistance" in this sentence. And yet, as in the sentence above, some doubt lingers as he makes this set of proclamations. Both protest and resistance characterize popular struggles, mass actions, and yet in this sentence, they characterize the critical capacities of a few. Adorno himself wavers slightly here even as he continues to clarify his speculative remarks, and he makes a slightly different claim for reflexivity: "dieser Widerstand gegen das, was die Welt aus uns gemacht hat, ist nun beileibe nicht bloss ein Unterschied gegen die äussere Welt . . . sondern dieser Widerstand müsste sich allerdings in uns selber gegen all das erweisen, worin wir dazu tendieren, mitzuspielen" ["This resistance to what the world has made of us does not at all imply merely an opposition to the external world on the grounds that we would be fully entitled to resist it. . . . In addition, we ought also to mobilize our own powers of resistance in order to resist those parts of us that are tempted to join in"].[13]

What Adorno might be said to rule out at such moments is the idea of popular resistance, of forms of critique that take shape as bodies amass on the street to articulate their opposition to contemporary regimes of power. But also, resistance is understood as a "no-saying" to the part of the self that wants to go along with (*mitzuspielen*) the status quo. It is understood both as a form of critique that only the elect few can undertake and as a resistance to a part of the self that seeks to join with what is wrong, an internal check against complicity. These claims limit the idea of resistance in ways that I myself would not finally be able to accept. For me, both claims prompt further questions: What part of the self is being refused, and what part is being empowered through resistance? If I refuse that part of myself that is complicit with the bad life, have I then made myself pure? Have I intervened to change the structure of that social world from which I withhold myself, or have I isolated myself? Have I joined with others in a movement of resistance and a struggle for social transformation?

These questions have, of course, been posed to Adorno's views for some time—I remember a demonstration in Heidelberg in 1979 when some groups on the left were contesting Adorno, protesting his limited idea of protest! For me, and perhaps for us today, we might still query in what way resistance must do more than refuse a way of life, a position that finally abstracts the moral from the political at the expense of solidarity, producing the very smart and morally pure critic as the model of resistance. If resistance is to enact the very principles of democracy for which it struggles, then resistance has to be *plural* and it has to be *embodied*. It will also entail the gathering of the ungrievable in public space, marking their existence and their demand for livable lives, the demand to live a life *prior* to death, simply put.

Indeed, if resistance is to bring about a new way of life, a more livable life that opposes the differential distribution of precarity, then acts of resistance will say no to one way of life at the same time that they say yes to another. For this purpose, we must reconsider for our times the performative consequences of concerted action in the Arendtian sense. Yet in my view, the concerted action that characterizes resistance is sometimes found in the verbal speech act or the heroic fight, but it is also found in those bodily gestures of refusal, silence, movement, and refusal to move that characterize those movements that enact democratic principles of equality and economic principles of interdependency in the very action by which they call for a new way of life that is more radically democratic and more substantially interdependent. A social movement is itself a social form, and when a social movement calls for a new way of life, a form of livable life, then it must, at that moment, enact the very principles it seeks to realize. This means that when it works, there is a performative enactment of radical democracy in such movements that alone can articulate what it might mean to lead a good life in the sense of a livable life. I have tried to suggest that precarity is the condition against which several new social movements struggle; such movements do not seek to overcome interdependency or even vulnerability as they struggle against precarity; rather, they seek to produce the conditions under which vulnerability and interdependency become livable. This is a politics in which performative action takes bodily and plural form, drawing critical attention to the conditions of bodily survival, persistence, and flourishing within the framework of radical democracy. If I am to lead a good life, it will be a life lived with others, a life that is no life without those others; I will not lose this *I* that I am; whoever I am will be transformed by my connections with others, since my dependency on another, and my dependability, are necessary in order to live and to live well. Our shared exposure to precarity is but one ground of our potential equality and our reciprocal obligations to produce together conditions of livable life. In avowing the need we have for one another, we avow as well basic principles that inform the social, democratic conditions of what we might still call "the good life." These are critical conditions of democratic life in the sense that they are part of an ongoing crisis, but also because they belong to a form of thinking and acting that responds to the urgencies of our time.

Notes

Introduction

1. Chantal Mouffe and Ernesto Laclau, *Hegemony and Socialist Strategy* (London: Verso, 1986).

2. Hamid Dabashi, *The Arab Spring: The End of Postcolonialism* (London: Zed Books, 2012).

3. Shoshana Felman, *The Scandal of the Speaking Body: Don Juan with J. L. Austin, or Seduction in Two Languages* (Palo Alto, CA: Stanford University Press, 2003).

4. Wendy Brown, "Neo-liberalism and the End of Liberal Democracy," *Theory and Event* 7, no. 1 (2003), accessed July 20, 2014, muse.jhu.edu /journals/theory_and_event/v007/7.1brown.html.

5. The notion of "disposable life" has emerged in a number of recent theoretical debates. See Achille Mbembe, "Necropolitics," *Public Culture* 15, no. 1 (2003): 11–40, and Beth Povinelli, *Economies of Abandonment* (Durham, NC: Duke University Press, 2011). See also the Columbia University website: http://historiesofviolence.com/specialseries/disposable-life/.

6. Michel Foucault, *Society Must Be Defended: Lectures at the Collège de France, 1975–76,* trans. David Macey (New York: Picador, 2002); Michel Foucault, *Security, Territory, Population: Lectures at the Collège de France, 1977–78,* trans. Graham Burchell (New York: Picador, 2009).

7. Isabell Lorey, *State of Insecurity: Government of the Precarious* (London: Verso, 2015).

8. Michel Feher, "Self-Appreciation; or, The Aspirations of Human Capital," *Public Culture* 21, no. 1 (2009): 21–41.

9. Lauren Berlant, *Cruel Optimism* (Durham, NC: Duke University Press, 2011).

10. Ibid.

11. Sheldon S. Wolin, "Fugitive Democracy," *Constellations: An International Journal of Critical and Democratic Theory* 1, no. 1 (1994): 11–25.

12. See my "Introduction: Precarious Life, Grievable Life," in *Frames of War: When Is Life Grievable?* (London: Verso, 2009).

1. Gender Politics and the Right to Appear

1. A chilling example of this refusal to heed the political demands implied by assembly took place in London in 2011, and also in the suburbs of Paris in 2005. See "Paul Gilroy Speaks on the Riots," *Dream of Safety* (blog), August 16, 2011, http://dreamofsafety.blogspot.com/2011/08/paul-gilroy -speaks-on-riots-august-2011.html. See also a number of recent reports on military personnel from Israel and Bahrain brought in to train local police how to suppress and disperse demonstrations: Max Blumenthal, "How Israeli Occupation Forces, Bahraini Monarchy Guards Trained U.S. Police for Coordinated Crackdown on 'Occupy' Protests," The Exiled, December 2, 2011, http://exiledonline.com/max-blumenthal-how-israeli-occupation-forces -bahraini-monarchy-guards-trained-u-s-police-for-coordinated-crackdown -on-occupy-protests/.

2. Jacques Derrida, "Signature Event Context," in *Limited Inc,* trans. Samuel Weber and Jeffrey Mehlman (Evanston, IL: Northwestern University Press, 1988); Pierre Bourdieu, *Language and Symbolic Power* (Cambridge, MA: Harvard University Press, 1991); Eve Kosofsky Sedgwick, *Epistemology of the Closet* (Berkeley: University of California Press, 1990).

3. In a Hegelian sense, the struggle for recognition never fully overcomes the life and death struggle.

4. See my *Frames of War* (London: Verso, 2010).

5. See Linda Zerilli, "The Arendtian Body," and Joan Cocks, "On Nationalism," in *Feminist Interpretations of Hannah Arendt,* ed. Bonnie Honig (University Park: Penn State University Press, 1995).

6. Hannah Arendt, *On Revolution* (New York: Penguin, 1963), 114.

7. Ibid.

8. Zerilli, "Arendtian Body," 178–179.

9. See Ruth Wilson Gilmore, *Golden Gulag: Prisons, Surplus, Crisis, and Opposition in Globalizing California* (Berkeley: University of California Press, 2007), 28.

10. For an account of how rights of bodily mobility are central to demo-cratic politics, see Hagar Kotef, *Movement and the Ordering of Freedom: On Liberal Governances of Mobility* (Durham, NC: Duke University Press, 2015).

11. Hannah Arendt, "The Decline of the Nation-State and the End of the Rights of Man," in *On Totalitarianism* (San Diego: Harcourt, Brace, Jo-vanovich, 1973), 267–302. See also Judith Butler and Gayatri Chakravorty Spivak, *Who Sings the Nation-State? Language, Politics, Belonging* (Calcutta: Seagull Books, 2007).

12. Joan W. Scott, *Politics of the Veil* (Princeton, NJ: Princeton Univer-sity Press, 2010).

13. See http://baltimore.cbslocal.com/2011/04/22/video-shows-woman -being-beaten-at-baltimore-co-mcdonalds/.

14. Palestinian Queers for Boycott, Divestment, and Sanctions, see http://www.pqbds.com/.

15. Jorge E. Hardoy and David Satterthwaite, *Squatter Citizen: Life in the Urban Third World* (London: Earthscan, 1989).

16. Denise Riley, *"Am I That Name?" Feminism and the Category of Women in History* (Minneapolis: University of Minnesota Press, 1988).

17. Eve Kosofksy Sedgwick, "Queer Performativity: Henry James's *The Art of the Novel,*" *GLQ* 1, no. 1 (1993): 1–16.

18. This final discussion is transposed from "Rethinking Vulnerability and Resistance," my lecture given in Alcala, Spain, in July 2014, part of which was published in the Modern Language Association's online journal, *Profession,* January 2014, https://profession.commons.mla.org/2014/03/19 /vulnerability-and-resistance/.

2. Bodies in Alliance and the Politics of the Street

1. Jasbir Puar, *Terrorist Assemblages: Homonationalism in Queer Times* (Durham, NC: Duke University Press, 2007).

2. Hannah Arendt, *The Human Condition* (Chicago: University of Chi-cago Press, 1958), 198.

3. Ibid.

4. Ibid., 199.

5. "The point of view of an ethics is: of what are you capable, what can you do? Hence a return to this sort of cry of Spinoza's: what can a body do? We never know in advance what a body can do. We never know how we're organized and how the modes of existence are enveloped in somebody." Gilles Deleuze, *Expressionism in Philosophy: Spinoza,* trans. Martin Joughin (New York: Zone Books, 1992), 217–234. This account differs from his in several respects, most prominently by virtue of its consideration of bodies

in their plurality, but also by asking, what are the conditions according to which a body can do anything at all?

6. Adriana Cavarero, *For More than One Voice: Toward a Philosophy of Vocal Expression,* trans. Paul A. Kottman (Palo Alto, CA: Stanford University Press, 2005).

7. Arendt, *Human Condition,* 199.

8. Giorgio Agamben, *Homo Sacer: Sovereign Power and Bare Life,* trans. Daniel Heller-Roazen (Palo Alto, CA: Stanford University Press, 1998).

9. Her first examination of the right to have rights in the context of refugees was in 1943, when she wrote "We, Refugees" in *The Menorah Journal.* See, also, Giorgio Agamben's brief commentary on this essay: http://round table.kein.org/node/399.

10. Zeynep Gambetti, "Occupy Gezi as Politics of the Body," in *The Making of a Protest Movement in Turkey,* ed. Umut Özkırımlı (Houndmills, Basingstoke: Palgrave Pivot, 2014).

11. Hans Wehr, *Dictionary of Modern Written Arabic,* 4th ed., ed. J. Milton Cowan (Ithaca, NY: Spoken Language Services, 1994), s.v. "salima."

12. Ruth Wilson Gilmore, *Golden Gulag: Prisons, Surplus, Crisis, and Opposition in Globalizing California* (Berkeley: University of California Press, 2007).

3. Precarious Life and the Ethics of Cohabitation

1. Susan Sontag, "Looking at War: Photography's View of Devastation and Death," in *Regarding the Pain of Others* (New York: Picador, 2003).

2. See my *Parting Ways: Jewishness and the Critique of Zionism* (New York: Columbia University Press, 2012), 23; and http://laphilosophie.blog .lemonde.fr/2013/03/21/levinas-trahi-la-reponse-de-judith-butler/. See also Levinas's remarks about the "Asiatic hordes" who threaten the ethical basis of Judeo-Christian culture in Emmanuel Levinas, "Jewish Thought Today," in *Difficult Freedom: Essays on Judaism,* trans. Sean Hand (Baltimore: Johns Hopkins University Press, 1990), 165. This is more fully discussed in my *Giving an Account of Oneself* (New York: Fordham University Press, 1995), 90–96.

3. See my *Parting Ways.*

4. Hannah Arendt, *Eichmann in Jerusalem: A Report on the Banality of Evil* (New York: Schocken Books, 1963), 277–278.

5. See Arendt's infamous letter to Karl Jaspers in 1961 in which she voices her disgust with Jews from Arab descent: "My first impression. On top, the judges, the best of German Jewry. Below them, the persecuting attorneys, Galicians, but still Europeans. Everything is organized by a police force that gives me the creeps, speaks only Hebrew and looks Arabic. Some down-

right brutal types among them. They would follow any order. And outside, the oriental mob, as if one were in Istanbul or some other half-Asiatic country. In addition, and very visible in Jerusalem, the peies and caftan Jews, who make life impossible for all the reasonable people here." See Hannah Arendt and Karl Jaspers, *Correspondence 1926–1969,* ed. Lotte Kohler and Hans Saner, trans. Robert and Rita Kimber (New York: Harcourt Brace Jovanovich, 1985), Letter 285, April 13, 1961, p. 435.

6. Meron Benvenisti, "The Binationalism Vogue," *Haaretz,* April 30, 2009, http://www.haaretz.com/print-edition/opinion/the-binationalism -vogue-1.275085.

4. Bodily Vulnerability, Coalitional Politics

1. It would be one matter to defend the rights of those with whom one disagrees to assemble on the street, and it would be another to celebrate or endorse the actual demonstrations. Although this essay does not address the conditions and limits of the right of assembly, it seems important to under-score from the start that I accept the right of all sorts of groups, including those with whom I most vehemently disagree, to assemble on the street. Although the right of assembly surely has its limits, my sense is that those limits would be at least partially and minimally established by demonstrating persuasively that a group deliberately poses a threat to the physical well-being of others who have an equal and legitimate claim to public space.

2. See Wendy Brown's work on the privatization of public goods, in-cluding "Neo-liberalism and the End of Liberal Democracy," *Theory and Event* 7, no. 1 (2003), accessed July 20, 2014, muse.jhu.edu/journals/theory _and_event/v007/7.1brown.html; and her remarks on privatization: http:// cupe3913.on.ca/wendy-brown-on-the-privatization-of-universities/.

3. Hannah Arendt, *The Human Condition* (Chicago: University of Chi-cago Press), 198.

4. Zeynep Gambetti, "Occupy Gezi as Politics of the Body," in *The Making of a Protest Movement in Turkey,* ed. Umut Özkırımlı (Houndmills, Basingstoke: Palgrave Pivot, 2014).

5. See "Posture Maketh the Man," in *The Richness of Life: The Essential Stephen J. Gould,* ed. Steven Rose (New York: Norton, 2007), 467–475.

6. This is a point made by Rosi Braidotti in her recent work, *The Post-human* (Cambridge: Polity, 2013), and Hélène Mialet in *Hawking Incorporated: Stephen Hawking and the Anthropology of the Knowing Subject* (Chicago: Uni-versity of Chicago Press, 2012).

7. See my "Introduction: Precarious Life, Grievable Life," in *Frames of War: When Is Life Grievable?* (London: Verso, 2009).

8. See Donna Haraway's views on complex relationalities in *Simians, Cyborgs, and Women: The Reinvention of Nature* (New York: Routledge, 1991) and in *The Companion Species Manifesto: Dogs, People, and Significant Otherness* (Chicago: Prickly Paradigm Press, 2003).

9. Feminist theorists on vulnerability are many, but a few recent articles give some sense of the important policy implications of this notion: Martha A. Fineman, "The Vulnerable Subject: Anchoring Equality in the Human Condition," *Yale Journal of Law and Feminism* 20, no. 1 (2008); Anna Grear, "The Vulnerable Living Order: Human Rights and the Environment in a Critical and Philosophical Perspective," *Journal of Human Rights and the Environment* 2, no. 1 (2011); Peadar Kirby, "Vulnerability and Globalization: Mediating Impacts on Society," *Journal of Human Rights and the Environment* 2, no. 1 (2011); Martha A. Fineman and Anna Grear, eds., *Vulnerability: Reflections on a New Ethical Foundation for Law and Politics* (Burlington, VT: Ashgate, 2013); and Katie E. Oliviero, "Sensational Nation and the Minutemen: Gendered Citizenship and Moral Vulnerabilities," *Signs: Journal of Women and Culture in Society* 32, no. 3 (2011). See also Bryan S. Turner, *Vulnerability and Human Rights* (University Park: Pennsylvania State University Press, 2006); and Shani D'Cruze and Anupama Rao, *Violence, Vulnerability and Embodiment: Gender and History* (Oxford: Blackwell, 2005).

10. For reflections on contemporary precarity, see Luc Boltanski and Eve Chiapello, *The New Spirit of Capitalism,* trans. Gregory Elliott (London: Verso, 2007).

11. The tactical deployment of the distinction between the vulnerable and the invulnerable depends as well on the differential allocation of permeability. The language of permeability became rather important in the United States after 9/11, referring to the permeability of national borders, drawing upon the anxieties of being entered against one's will, the invasion of bodily boundaries. Both sexual interdictions and gender norms are at work in such language, to be sure—the fear of rape, the prerogative to rape, to name but a few ways in which gendered differences are established through the political problems raised by the permeability of the body, a condition that can only be managed, but not escaped (since all bodies have orifices, or can be pierced by instruments). And yet, the impossible project goes on by which one gender is regarded as permeable and the other not.

12. Albert Memmi, *Dependence: A Sketch for a Portrait of the Dependent,* trans. Philip A. Facey (Boston: Beacon Press, 1984).

13. See Gilles Deleuze, "What Can a Body Do?" in *Expressionism in Philosophy: Spinoza,* trans. Martin Joughin (New York: Zone Books, 1992).

14. See Isabelle Stengers, *Thinking with Whitehead: A Free and Wild Creation of Concepts,* trans. Michael Chase (Cambridge, MA: Harvard University Press, 2011).

15. As public and courageous a takeover of public space as they were, Slut Walks were also usefully criticized by black women for not understanding the impossibility of reappropriating the term "slut." See "An Open Letter from Black Women to the SlutWalk," *Black Women's Blueprint Blog,* September 23, 2011, http://www.blackwomensblueprint.org/2011/09/23/an-open-letter-from-black-women-to-the-slutwalk/.

16. Bernice Johnson Reagon, "Coalition Politics: Turning the Century," in *Home Girls: A Black Feminist Anthology,* ed. Barbara Smith (New York: Kitchen Table: Women of Color Press, 1983), 356–357.

5. "We the People"—Thoughts on Freedom of Assembly

1. The International Labour Organization makes clear that the right to freedom of peaceable assembly is central to collective bargaining and participation and membership in international labor organizations. See David Tajgman and Karen Curtis, *Freedom of Association: A User's Guide—Standards, Principles, and Procedures of the International Labour Organization* (Geneva: International Labour Office, 2000), 6. The United Nations, in its "Universal Declaration of Human Rights" (1948), specifies the right of assembly in articles 20 and 23. Perhaps most importantly, the International Covenant on Civil and Political Rights (1976) confirms the principle as it is formulated by the ILO, renaming it as a right of association and a right to organize in article 22: http://www.ohchr.org/en/professionalinterest/pages/ccpr.aspx.

2. This tends to be the focus of Giorgio Agamben's account of state sovereignty in *State of Exception,* trans. Kevin Attell (Chicago: University of Chicago Press, 2005).

3. Although Arendt does not address freedom of assembly directly in *On Revolution,* she does track the way that those who emerged, enraged about suffering, on the street during the French Revolution became the masses for whom vengeance was the primary aim (*On Revolution* [London: Penguin Books, 1965], 110–111). Their aim to liberate themselves from suffering was not the same as the proper aim of freedom, in her view. Freedom involves acting in concert to produce the new and, in political terms, to produce the new on the ground of equality. In her view, the task is to move from vengeance to an "act of founding the new body politic" (a movement that echoes Nietzsche's effort to prod those who practice slave morality to find resources for affirmation) (ibid., 222–223). One finds her drawing on

Tocquevillian notions of "voluntary association" in her essay "Civil Disobedience," in *Crises of the Republic* (New York: Harcourt Brace Jovanovich, 1972), 49–102. It is significant that the only discussion in that text referencing "assembly" is to the "constituent assembly" understood as the national assembly. It is Jason Frank who finds the "constituent power" in the freedom of assembly, which he finds to have different valence in Arendt's work depending on whether she is analyzing the French or American revolutions (Jason Frank, *Constituent Moments: Enacting the People in Postrevolutionary America* [Durham, NC: Duke University Press, 2010], 62–66). See also Seyla Benhabib, *The Reluctant Modernism of Hannah Arendt* (Oxford: Rowman and Littlefield, 2000), 123–129.

4. John D. Inazu, *Liberty's Refuge, The Forgotten Freedom of Assembly* (New Haven, CT: Yale University Press, 2012). Inazu writes that freedom of assembly has to be separated from freedom of association and the right of expressive association: "something important is lost when we fail to grasp the connection between a group's formation, composition, and existence and its expression. Many group expressions are only intelligible against the lived practices that give them meaning" (2).

5. See J. Kēhaulani Kauanui, *Hawaiian Blood: Colonialism and the Politics of Sovereignty and Indigeneity* (Durham, NC: Duke University Press, 2008).

6. Frank, *Constituent Moments*.

7. Ernesto Laclau, *On Populist Reason* (London: Verso, 2005), 65–128.

8. The relation of these remarks to the Deleuzian notion of assemblage is considered in Naomi Greyser, "Academic and Activist Assemblages: An Interview with Jasbir Puar," in *American Quarterly* 64, no. 4 (December 2012): 841–843.

9. In this respect, consider "the standing man," Erdem Gunduz, who defied the prohibition on assembly by standing alone in the square only then to be accompanied by others who stood alone until a veritable assembly of singular individuals had arrived, standing and silent, obeying and defying the prohibition at once: https://www.youtube.com/watch?v=SldbnzQ3nfM; Emma Sinclair-Webb, "The Turkish Protests—Still Standing," Human Rights Watch, June 21, 2013, http://www.hrw.org/news/2013/06/21/turkish-protests-still-standing.

10. Banu Bargu, "Spectacles of Death: Dignity, Dissent, and Sacrifice in Turkey's Prisons," in *Policing and Prisons in the Middle East: Formations of Coercion,* eds. Laleh Khalili and Jillian Schwedler (New York: Columbia University Press, 2010), 241–261; and Banu Bargu, "Fasting unto Death: Necropolitical Resistance in Turkey's Prisons" (manuscript form).

11. Angela Davis, *Are Prisons Obsolete?* (New York: Seven Stories Press, 2003), and Angela Davis, *Abolition Democracy: Beyond Empire, Prisons, and Torture* (New York: Seven Stories Press, 2005).

12. Frank, *Constituent Moments,* 33.

13. Agnes Heller, *The Theory of Need in Marx* (London: Allison and Busby, 1974).

14. See Wendy Brown's successive critiques of privatization: "Sacrificial Citizenship: Neoliberal Austerity Politics," http://globalization.gc.cuny.edu /events/sacrificial-citizenship-neoliberal-austerity-politics/; "The End of Educated Democracy," in *The Humanities and the Crisis of the Public University,* ed. Colleen Lie, Christopher Newfield, and James Vernon, special issue, *Representations* 116, no. 1 (Fall 2011): 19–41; "Neoliberalized Knowledge," *History of the Present* 1, no. 1 (May 2011); and *Undoing the Demos: Neoliberalism's Stealth Revolution* (New York: Zone Books, 2015).

15. See Mahatma Gandhi, *Selected Political Writings* (Indianapolis, IN: Hackett, 1996). Gandhi distinguished between passive resistance and nonviolent civil disobedience. In his view, passive resistance is a tactic ungoverned by a principle, whereas nonviolence is a form of action that is governed by principle and seeks to be consistent under all circumstances. He associated passive resistance with the powers of the weak, whereas, in his view, nonviolent civil disobedience is "intense activity" and "strength" (50–52).

16. M. K. Gandhi, *Non-violent Resistance (Satyagraha)* (Mineola, NY: Dover Publications, 2001), 2.

6. Can One Lead a Good Life in a Bad Life?

1. Theodor W. Adorno, *Minima Moralia: Reflections from Damaged Life,* trans. E. F. N. Jephcott, (London: New Left Books, 1974), 39.

2. Theodor W. Adorno, *Probleme der Moralphilosophie* (Frankfurt: Suhrkamp, 1996), 34–35; Adorno, *Problems of Moral Philosophy,* trans. Rodney Livingstone (Palo Alto, CA: Stanford University Press, 2002), 19 (hereafter cited as *PMP*).

3. Ibid., 205; *PMP,* 138.

4. Ibid., 262; *PMP,* 176.

5. Ibid., 250; *PMP,* 169.

6. Orlando Patterson, *Slavery and Social Death: A Comparative Study* (Cambridge, MA: Harvard University Press, 1985).

7. In "The Jewish Army—The Beginning of Jewish Politics?" published in *Aufbau* (1941), Arendt writes, "The Jewish will to live is both famous and infamous. Famous because it spans a relatively long period in the history of

European peoples. Infamous, because over the last two hundred years it had threatened to degenerate into something totally negative: the will to survive at any price." *Jewish Writings,* eds. Jerome Kohn and Ron H. Feldman (New York: Schocken, 2007), 137. In 1946, as the full horror of the Nazi concentration camps was still being revealed and the political outcome of Zionism was still actively debated, she revisits this point in "The Jewish State: Fifty Years After, Where Have Herzl's Politics Led?" There she writes, "What the survivors now want above all else is the right to die with dignity— in case of attack, with weapons in their hands. Gone, probably forever, is that chief concern of the Jewish people for centuries: survival at any price. Instead, we find something essentially new among Jews, the desire for dignity at any price." She then continues, "As great an asset as this new development would be to an essentially sane Jewish political movement, it nevertheless constitutes something of a danger within the present framework of Zionist attitudes. Herzl's doctrine, deprived as it now is of its original confidence in the helpful nature of anti-Semitism, can only encourage suicidal gestures for whose ends the natural heroism of people who have become accustomed to death can be easily exploited" (386).

8. Hannah Arendt, "The Answer of Socrates," in *The Life of the Mind,* vol. 1 (New York: Harcourt, 1977), 168–178.

9. Hannah Arendt, *Zwischen Vergangenheit und Zukunft: Übungen im politischen Denken 1,* ed. Ursula Ludz (München: Piper, 1994), 44f.

10. On complex relationalities, see Donna Haraway, *Simians, Cyborgs, and Women: The Reinvention of Nature* (New York: Routledge, 1991); and *The Companion Species Manifesto: Dogs, People, and Significant Otherness* (Chicago: Prickly Paradigm Press, 2003).

11. Adorno, *Probleme der Moralphilosophie,* 248; *PMP,* 167.

12. Ibid., 249; *PMP,* 167–168.

13. Ibid; *PMP,* 168.

Acknowledgments

I would like first to thank Bryn Mawr College for hosting me in 2010 to give the Mary Flexner Lectures, especially those faculty and students who engaged the work intensively, and former president Jane McAuliffe, who extended this invitation so graciously and whose impressive staff made my stay both easy and productive. I would like to thank all those at Harvard University Press for their patience in waiting for the final version of this text, and the Andrew Mellon Foundation for supporting me with the Distinguished Academic Achievement Award during the time I developed these lectures, transformed them into chapters, and sought to sew them together in book form. The present book emerges from conversations and joint projects with similar scholars and activists working on questions of political assembly, precarity, and resistance. Chapters 1, 2, and 4 began as lectures that I gave at Bryn Mawr. Those then emerged in different forms as I prepared them for new occasions. I thank as well my interlocutors at Boğaziçi University, who offered generous criticism of Chapter 5, "We the People," in 2013, a few months after the Gezi demonstrations. I am grateful to the audience at the Watson Lecture at the Nobel Museum in Stockholm in 2011, who responded helpfully to the first version of "The Ethics of Cohabitation," and to the Venice Biennale, where an early version of "Bodies in Alliance and the Politics of the Street" was presented in 2010. "Can One Lead a Good Life in a Bad Life?" was presented in Frankfurt on the occasion of receiving the Adorno Prize in September 2012.

I thank Sarah Bracke and Aleksey Dubilet for their invaluable assistance with the manuscript, both intellectual and textual. I thank Lindsay Waters for prompting and shepherding this book along, and Amanda Peery for all her help. As always, I am most happily indebted to my interlocutors, those who are most proximate, those I rarely see, and those I have yet to meet. I thank Wendy Brown, my most proximate person, who has supported and challenged this work with invaluable attention and just the right amount of distance. I thank as well my other readers, whose productive quarrels and exceptional questions have been invaluable: Michel Feher, Leticia Sabsay, Zeynep Gambetti, Michelle Ty, Amy Huber, Alex Chasin, and my anonymous readers, all of whom proved to be exceptionally good company when doubts started to gather and it became time to disperse these speculations, however overdue, however premature. This book is dedicated to Isaac Butler-Brown, who has already learned to show up, to speak out.

Credits

Chapter 2, "Bodies in Alliance and the Politics of the Street," has been expanded for this volume from a text that appeared first in *Sensible Politics: The Visual Culture of Nongovernmental Activism,* ed. Meg McLagan and Yates McKee (New York: Zone Books, 2012), 117–138.

Chapter 3, "Precarious Life and the Ethics of Cohabitation," was first presented as the Watson Lecture at the Nobel Museum in Stockholm in 2011 and was originally published in slightly different form as "Precarious Life, Vulnerability, and the Ethics of Cohabitation" in the *Journal of Speculative Philosophy* 26, no. 2 (2012): 134–151.

Chapter 4, "Bodily Vulnerability, Coalitional Politics," was first published as "Bodily Vulnerability, Coalitions, and Street Politics" in *Differences in Common: Gender, Vulnerability, Community,* ed. Joana Sabadell-Nieto and Marta Segarra (Amsterdam/New York: Rodopi Publishing, 2014).

Chapter 6, "Can One Lead a Good Life in a Bad Life?" was first presented in Frankfurt on the occasion of receiving the Adorno Prize in September 2012 and was first published in *Radical Philosophy* 176 (November/December 2012).

Index